# IN SEARCH OF
# Centennial
## A JOURNEY WITH JAMES A. MICHENER

## by John Kings

### INTRODUCTION BY JAMES A. MICHENER

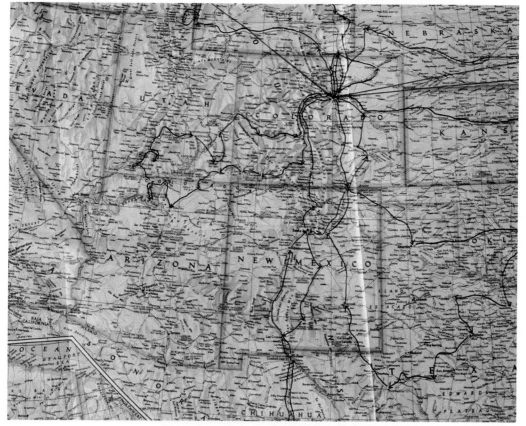

With Photographs by
Tessa Dalton, James A. Michener, and the author

RANDOM HOUSE

NEW YORK

AN ORIGINAL VOLUME FROM

VISUAL BOOKS Inc.

342 MADISON AVENUE, NEW YORK, N.Y. 10017

The photographs on page 16
and on pages 19-39 inclusive
are © James A. Michener.
Unless otherwise stated, all
other photographs are © John Kings.

Library of Congress Cataloging in Publication Data
Kings, John, 1923-
    In search of Centennial.
    Includes index.
    1. Michener, James Albert, 1907-    Centennial.
I. Title
PS3525.I19C434          813'.5'4          78-14389
ISBN 0-394-50292-2

Manufactured in the United States of America
Printed and Bound by
Rose Printing Company Inc., Tallahassee, Florida

# CONTENTS

Introduction_____7
Preface_____11
THE ORIGINS OF *CENTENNIAL*_____17
THE LONG JOURNEYS_____40
DENVER AND THE SHORT FORAYS_____68
THE WRITING_____95
THE FILM_____112
Appendix_____136
Index_____142

James A. Michener in Colorado. He had completed the first

draft of *Centennial* when this picture was taken in May, 1973 ( Photo © Tessa Dalton)

*I am a galley slave*
*to pen and ink.*

Honoré de Balzac
*Lettres, 1832*

# INTRODUCTION

Reading *In Search of Centennial* gave me double pleasure. Since I had been personally involved in the long and complicated research that accompanied the writing of the novel *Centennial*, John Kings' accurate and truthful account of its genesis covers ground with which I was already familiar. But since it was told by another participant, it gave me the pleasure of being reminded of some nearly forgotten events, seen through eyes other than my own. (Incidentally, friends who have long wanted me to dress like a proper British author, with pipe and tweed, will be amused by Mr. Kings' accurate description of my working garb.)

For readers who are unfamiliar with what goes into the making of a long and complex novel, this book should prove informative as well as agreeable. And the intricacies involved in constructing a long television film based on a novel may be fascinating and bewildering, as they were to me.

What gave me perhaps the most personal satisfaction was, however, to find that some of the photographs I had made in the west forty-two years ago were still suitable for use as illustrations in this book today. They demonstrate forcefully the point that a novelist builds his work over very long periods of time. An illumination achieved in 1936 may not be utilized until four decades later.

*James A. Michener*

July 1978
Maryland

Long, lonely roads, this one in Texas, took us back to the
beginnings of man's western story. (Photo © Tessa Dalton)

The wagons took six months to cover 2,000 miles.

We travelled 25,000 miles in three months in search of Centennial; here heading south from New to Old Mexico.

*For*
*TARKA*

## ACKNOWLEDGEMENTS

I would like to thank James A. Michener for making available to me his records on the writing of *Centennial,* for giving me permission to quote freely from them and to select illustrations from them; and for the time he took, in Colorado, New York and London, to discuss various aspects of his working methods. The meetings were both enjoyable and instructive.

My thanks to Random House Inc. for permission to use extracts from *Centennial;* from their privately circulated volume, *About Centennial,* by James A. Michener; and to quote briefly from *The Drifters,* and *The Bridges at Toko-Ri.* I also thank Albert Erskine for his perceptive overlook of the manuscript; and Miss Bert Krantz.

To the staff of the James A. Michener Library, at the University of Northern Colorado, Greeley, Colorado, and especially to Mr. Gabor Kovacs, Assistant Director of the library, I am most grateful for their assistance and kindness during my many visits; and to the Panhandle Plains Museum, University of West Texas, Canyon, Texas, for permission to reproduce items from their collection.

For material incorporated in the chapter on the filming of *Centennial,* I am grateful for co-operation from film crew members of Universal Inc.; and from John Wilder, Virgil Vogel, Howard Alston, Susan Lichwardt, Mack Harding and Janice Welch. They initiated me into a few of the mysteries of film making.

I thank Nicolas Ducrot of Visual Books Inc., for his enthusiastic support of the project, and for his imaginative interpretation in the book's design; also Jayne Lathrop.

Finally, I would like to thank Hobart Lewis for giving me the original assignment to work with James A. Michener on *Centennial;* my good neighbors in Big Horn, Wyoming, for holding the fort during my long absences from home; and Christy Love, for her frequent help, and that most essential of all ingredients, encouragement.

*Ne tentes aut perfice*

# PREFACE

he year I spent with James Michener in the preparation of *Centennial* is etched clearly and indelibly in my memory. Scarcely a day passes without some facet of those months returning to mind, a sure indication of the intensity of the experience, for it has to compete with recollections of other vivid and absorbing periods of my life. Yet neither North Sea duties in the Royal Navy during World War II, nor the challenge of an entirely unaccustomed way of life as a cattle rancher among the grandeur of Wyoming's Big Horn mountains, from 1966–72, can match for sheer exhilaration the stimulus I felt in working with Michener on *Centennial*.

The twenty years between the episodes of the sea and the mountains gave me writing and editing experience in book and magazine publishing in London and New York, and it was the unlikely combination of editing and cattle ranching that led to my assignment.

In September 1972, no longer sitting easy in the saddle in my ranching endeavours, I was covering an international convention of parks' directors for *Reader's Digest* magazine when Hobart Lewis, the *Digest's* editor-in-chief, telephoned. Would I like to work with James Michener in the preparation of a major novel on the west? He had told Michener of my dual life as a rancher/editor with knowledge of western history, and had suggested that I might be especially helpful for those parts of the manuscript dealing with the development of the cattle industry.

When I hung up the phone my mind was quickly diverted from the natural wonders of the Snake River. The assignment was intriguing, even alarming, for my only awareness of Michener, gained randomly from others over the years and in no way based on first-hand knowledge, was of a difficult man, a martinet whom it was almost impossible to please.

This impression was not reversed at our first meeting in Denver, for though he was courteous, there seemed to be little warmth to balance his austere, almost severe approach to the task in hand. With me, at Hobart Lewis's bidding, was an English

*Centennial* country, Colorado.

researcher/photographer, Tessa Dalton, who had lived in Denver for the previous five years and could be helpful on the Colorado sections of the novel. Also at the meeting was Michener's friendly wife, Mari, who obviously played a very helpful part in her husband's day-to-day activities.

Michener outlined the scope of his proposed novel — it had no title at that time — chapter by chapter, and told us his basic plans for its preparation. He explained to Tessa that her research duties would include a role as photographer to secure a visual record of the making of the book, a task for which she was well equipped. My job would be as a researcher/editor/driver, with particular emphasis on ranch life.

At the conclusion of that first meeting Michener gave us our first assignment — to go to Pennsylvania and reconstruct a day-by-day journey of a wagon and flatboat journey from Lancaster to St. Louis, undertaken by two young migrants in 1844. Meanwhile, in Denver, he would continue wrestling with the problems of earth's creation and the coming of the dinosaur. Lastly he reminded us that although we would be working very hard, we would also have a lot of fun. Of the hard work I had absolutely no doubt, but the possibility of any light relief along the way seemed, at that moment, to be remote.

And so it came about, by an unlikely and circuitous route, that two English transplants were retained to assist in the research and preparation of the definitive novel of the west, to be written by that most indigenous of American authors, James A. Michener. I learned much later that our co-operation on this project would be as new an experience for Michener as it would be for me. Never before had he retained any full-time help in the preparation of a novel — other than from his wife, Mari, and from Nadia Orapchuk, his wonderfully ebullient super-secretary in his native Pennsylvania. Nor had I ever worked, over a protracted period, on a day-to-day basis with any author — let alone with Michener of such fierce repute. I was thrilled at this opportunity to contribute to the preparation of a novel on those western lands I had grown to love, to be written by a man so obviously determined to seek out the truths of his subject. For his part Michener wrote crisply to Hobart Lewis: "We have met with the two English people and find them delightful prospects for constructive work. Look much better than average. We are all at work."

During that year, from October 1972 through October 1973, we travelled together by car more than 25,000 miles in search of *Centennial,* peeling layers of history from the land, probing for truths in an area that is heavily overlaid with sentimental and nostalgic myth. We were not out to glorify historical pygmies like Butch Cassidy or Billy the Kid, we were seeking concrete facts to portray accurately that mainstream settling of the eastern face of the Rockies, and particularly that area between the North and South Platte rivers where the high plains finally break against the mountain ramparts of Colorado and Wyoming.

We were after the backbreak and the heartbreak, the triumphs and tragedies, and the everyday lives, of a cavalcade of astonishingly diverse humanity which played out the drama of the west over a period of two hundred years. In the course of that search we drove by car through fourteen states and into old Mexico, and while doing so we kept a record, both in words and pictures, of our progress. The end result was the collection of material that Michener fashioned into his best-selling novel on the west, and perhaps his best beloved, for he was writing at last of his homeland, and of a part of it that had been extraordinarily significant in his own life.

Michener had lived in the flatlands of Colorado during the Great Depression, and the memories of those harsh years had stayed with him. Yet, even more than that, his undiminished affection for the lands of the Platte had persisted through the years, so that in the writing of this novel he was often exposing raw nerve ends. During our journeys he was always the professional, detached researcher on the surface, but there was a strong undercurrent of deep personal involvement. To one site, the abandoned township of Keota, east of Greeley, he would go back six, seven, even twelve times, sometimes merely to stand in momentary isolation from us, tuned in once again to those currents in Colorado's turbulent history that had affected him so deeply nearly forty years earlier.

During our journeys I found that people had an almost abiding curiosity about James Michener. Whenever a community learned that he was in town the reaction was invariably the same — an overriding desire to meet him, to talk with him. In Cody, Wyoming, for example, the town librarian discovered that we were working on research at the Buffalo Bill Historical Center. Immediately the request was straight to the point. Would Mr. Michener please come to the library that evening to give a short talk? It was scant notice indeed, but Jim Michener is a pushover for libraries, so he readily agreed, the local radio station made hourly announcements of the event throughout the day, and the bush telegraph was hot. By the time we reached the library it was packed to the doors. People of all ages had driven in from a large surrounding area, from as far distant as 120 miles, to question him about his work, his beliefs, his plans for the future. All of this from an agricultural community as yet totally unaware of a forthcoming book that would touch deeply on their own heritage. They were there because of *The Fires of Spring,* or *The Source, Hawaii, Iberia* and *The Drifters.* They were there because Michener's books had in one way or another touched their lives far beyond the mere extent of their storytelling.

Simply put, the Michener mystique, and there certainly is one, is a very strong drawcard, perhaps, above all, because he is able as a writer to remind us of the essential values that go to the making of a healthy society.

This book, then, is in response to countless requests from Michener readers for an insight into the way he works, and the manner of the man. My purpose is to give an idea of what went into the making of *Centennial,* the only area of his work about which I can write with personal knowledge. The preparation of this volume was finally prompted when I learned that Universal intended to produce a 25-hour television version of the book, for NBC. It seemed an appropriate moment to record these comments.

With some trepidation I bounced the idea off Jim, essentially a secret man averse to biographical exposure. Perhaps he would not want me to re-create that working year on *Centennial?* To the contrary, he immediately agreed that such an account could provide a long-desired insight for his readers. "You have my blessing," he said without hesitation, and added generously, "and you can have access to all the files and research on the book."

I am indebted to him. For his permission, for his continuing encouragement, and most of all for that rewarding year spent with him in the preparation of *Centennial.* And, yes, he was right. We did have a lot of fun along the way.

Big Horn, Wyoming

# CHAPTER I

# THE ORIGINS OF CENTENNIAL

O<sup></sup>n April 7, 1970, James Michener tapped the following passage on his typewriter:

*7.IV.70*

*This morning I woke up with a
complete novel outlined. I had
not thought of its subject since
1937, but now it stood forth in
complete detail.*

*The background, I suppose, is
that many people have been
after me to write about the
United States, Helen Strauss and
Hobart Lewis among my immediate
friends, scores of my correspondents.*

*Also, the Centennial Commission
has been having some private meetings
with me on the subject of our nation's
two hundredth birthday, and I've
been poring over the secret report
to the President, helping to draft
certain sections.*

*The word Centennial must have reminded
me of the Centennial State, and of an
imaginary plains town of that name
which has lived with me since 1937
when I first saw the Platte, mighty
and grubby river.*

Michener then cut it from the sheet of paper and pasted it neatly into the top left-hand corner of a new notebook, the first of many he would fill during the progress of the novel over the next three and a half years.

Two things about that passage are characteristic. One, that on waking he went immediately to his typewriter and began to outline the concept, for one of Michener's inviolable self-disciplines is that he never wastes time. For him, the five days of the week, as well as week-ends, festivals, birthdays, Christmas, Easter, Super Bowl day are all grist to the mill if he is within range of a typewriter. Even to break for lunch is about as welcome a diversion as a pit stop in the Indianapolis 500.

Second, and another example of the discipline and order that are absolute corner-

17

In the late 1930's Michener explored the lands
he returned to write about forty years later.

In the forty years since Michener took this photograph, these buttes have weathered fractionally. In another forty they will erode a little more, but essentially they will remain the same as they have been through recorded time, a backdrop against which Indian and white man played out the story of the west.

Michener's interest in Indian heritage was kindled at Mesa Verde, Colorado during a visit in 1936. The catalyst was a book named *The Delight Makers*, by Francis Alphonse Bandlier. *'I read it in the ruins of what had once been an Indian metropolis—a delicate perceptive re-creation of an Indian culture.* (Photo © Tessa Dalton)

stones of Michener's approach to writing, is that having committed his waking idea to paper, he at once transferred it to the neat confines of a notebook — his methodical way of assembling material as a project develops.

The year he mentions, 1937, was the second of three consecutive years that he spent in Greeley, Colorado, as Director of Social Studies at the Colorado State College of Education, later to become the University of Northern Colorado. His coming to Colorado was in a sense anti-climactic. By 1936, at twenty-nine years of age, he had attended eight universities at home and overseas, including Harvard, St. Andrews, Scotland, and Siena, Italy, and had emerged from all with distinction.

That summer of 1936, with a reputation as something of an educational whiz-kid, he attended a session at Ohio State University and made known his Colorado plans for the following year. Invited to explain his intentions before the Ohio State faculty, Michener was told that he was about to throw away his career on a useless sojourn in the barbaric west, that his decision was the greatest mistake he could possibly make. One sage member summed up the sentiments of the appalled faculty in a heartrending oration Michener well remembers. "The sands of the desert are white with the bones of young men who went west and are trying to get back east," he intoned.

For Michener, the exact opposite proved true. He found in the west a whole new way of life to intrigue and fascinate him, and experienced a sense of freedom to think and move that resulted in three of the most determining years of his life. "At Greeley, I grew up spiritually, emotionally and intellectually," he says. By 1938, far from lying bleached in the desert sun, his reputation was further enhanced and he was besieged with offers from several universities, both east and west, including Stanford and Harvard. He chose Harvard, as a visiting professor during 1939–40.

The time he spent in Greeley forged a bond with the west that remained strong throughout his writing career, and the distant horizons of Colorado finally reclaimed him on April 7, 1970. One of the factors in Michener's decision to write a novel of the west stemmed from his concern with the upcoming Bicentennial celebration. He looked on it as an opportunity for the nation to renew its spiritual strength through some tangible and imaginative gesture that would serve as a continuing reminder of its founding values. Since 1969 he had been involved with the President's Committee set up to suggest appropriate ways of marking the occasion.

One by one Michener saw imaginative and far-reaching concepts eroded by short-sighted legislators who basically envisioned July 4, 1976, as a date for little more than a souped-up carnival. For nine months Michener had been "contributing to a vision of a true bicentennial, and to see it perish so ignobly hurt." His brooding frustration, as a result, stirred his own memories of his country, and triggered the idea for a novel that would span a period of 200 years.

"The grand design was dead," he wrote, "and it occurred to me that the best we could hope for would be for each citizen in our country to assume responsibility for his or her own bicentennial celebration.

"Once I realized this my responsibility became clear. I would use my knowledge of my nation and write about its spiritual condition as honestly as I could. My vehicle would be the western novel I had contemplated for so long."

Michener's decision to begin work on his own bicentennial project coincided with growing pressure from his agent, publishers, and readers that he divert his attention from overseas subjects in favor of a domestic setting and theme. It also came at a time in his writing career at which he was fully equipped to meet the challenges such a sweeping concept presented.

Once before, around 1950, he had begun work on a western novel, and had completed the first hundred or so pages before abandoning it. Until that date he had published, at book length, only *South Pacific* and that sensitive story reflective of his own youth, *The Fires of Spring*. It is not surprising that he was tempted to continue presenting facets of his own life, in this instance the experiences of a young school-teacher, albeit a young woman, in the imaginary state of Jefferson, clearly patterned after Colorado; and with the fictional school town of Livermore doubling for Greeley.

But he put it aside. "I cannot say why I dropped the idea; I have always played around with multiple ideas and gone fairly far into plots before concluding that they were not as promising as I had thought originally. This could have been a splendid portrait of a young woman in the west and I have never forgotten the ideas I associated with the theme. They were to come to fruition later — a quarter of a century later."

So he put the idea aside, and returned instead to the South Pacific as inspiration for his next book, *Return to Paradise*. Many of his basic concepts for *Jefferson* were still valid when he examined his thoughts for *Centennial*. The paramount factor missing in 1950 was his ability to handle the subject to its best advantage, and I believe that, intuitively, he recognized that.

*Jefferson* was to cover a period between 1936 and 1946, and his outline shows that in that brief span he intended to include chapters on many of the subjects that reappeared in *Centennial*: The Plains, Woman on the Plains, Mexicans, Sugar Beets, The Sheriff, Irrigation were all there. He put a great deal of preliminary work into the novel and then turned away from it, but the images remained, strengthened, if anything, over the years, became refined, expanded, and woven into a time frame twenty times longer than the mere decade he had chosen for *Jefferson*.

Although he abandoned that early novel, Michener showed his interest in the Rocky Mountain region in many stories he wrote before *Centennial*. The scene of a book might be Europe, the Far East or the South Pacific, but wherever it was set, the characters often revealed a Colorado background or had been deeply impressed by the west.

References to Colorado and particularly to Denver in his earlier books are constant. In *Tales of the South Pacific*, Ensign Bill Harbison played basketball in the Mountain States, lived in Denver, and married a girl from Albuquerque, New Mexico. While stationed in the South Pacific, Harbison's reading material consisted of *Time, Life,* and the *Denver Post*.

In *The Bridges at Toko-Ri,* the hero, Harry Brubaker, leaves a law practice, a wife and two daughters in Denver to fly fighter jets for the Air Force in Korea. Brubaker is very bitter about this separation: *"It would be easier to take if people back home were helping. But in Denver nobody even knew there was a war except my wife. Nobody supports this war."*

In *Sayonara,* the secretary of the American consul in Japan is married to an American soldier from Denver. The secretary explains to Ace Gruver that her husband chose her rather than a Japanese girl because he decided she would *"fit in better in Denver."*

In *The Drifters,* Joe, a bright college dropout/draft dodger, is greatly moved by the Wyoming landscape as he travels to the east coast to leave the United States. Joe is impressed by the same vast and endless landscape that had so affected Michener as a college professor in Greeley: *"His first moment of grandeur — the excitement he sought — came later when he crossed the vast and barren wastes of Wyoming. The road swept eastward in noble curves through mountains and across limitless*

A late 1930's Michener shot of boiling skies threatening the Colorado plains. The Burma Shave sign attests to the era, the indigo clouds recall the great duststorms that destroyed the lands beneath them. *And the duststorms kept returning, one after another, in high billowing grandeur, sweeping the world before them.*—Chapter 13, *Drylands*

The wide flatland which Michener grew to love more than the mountain peaks. He admired the high country for its grandeur, but was most in harmony with the Colorado landscape when we were criss-crossing the prairies from one barren horizon to another. *The vast plains had a nobility that would never diminish, for they were a challenge, with their duststorms, their wild blizzards, their tornadoes and their endless promise, if men treated them with respect . . . They were a resource inexhaustible in their variety but demanding in their love.*—Chapter 3, *The Inhabitants*

*plains. He travelled fifty or sixty miles at a clip without seeing so much as a gasoline station, and the occasional tiny town looked like a steer strayed from the herd and lost in the immensity of sky and wasteland."* During the snowstorm east of Rawlins, Joe is left with such an affinity for the vastness of the west that he knows he will one day return. As did Jim Michener.

During his three years in Colorado, Michener gained an intimate knowledge of the land, roaming the mountains and the plains in his determination to understand the natural and human elements that had created the patterns of history along the eastern slopes of the Rockies. He carried those images with him through the years, partly as a result of a remarkable series of photographs he took at that time.

He was encouraged to use a camera by a Greeley newspaper editor, Floyd Merrill, who took him on expeditions in the surrounding countryside. Merrill fired Michener's imagination. "At least three times each month Merrill and I went on excursions out of Greeley, sometimes to the intricate irrigation systems which made our part of the desert a garden of melons, sometimes to glens far above timberline, from which we would look down into valleys crowded with blue spruce and aspen, and quite often out onto the prairie east of town where majestic buttes rose starkly from the barren waste."

Michener came back from those sorties with a sensitive and poetic series of photographs that have survived the years. When I came upon them I feared that 1936–7 Kodachrome slides would have lost their colors, but they were in remarkably good condition. A number of them are reproduced in this book, moody, beautiful shots taken by a discerning eye preoccupied with those same images that later formed the nucleus of *Centennial*. ". . . in 1936 and 1937, during the years of the great duststorms, I had caught on film a percentage of the images I would later use in my novel. Here are the drylands that break men's hearts; here is the little town not yet dead but clearly dying; here are the deerlike Tarahumare Indians in the city of Chihuahua down in old Mexico; here is the look of the land I would be writing about one day. If those images persisted on film, they persisted in my mind with treble clarity."

These photographs, and Floyd Merrill's correspondence from Colorado through the years after Michener came back east, were continuing and vital reminders of his western experience. "Almost everything I wrote about in the novel had been earlier defined by me, and carefully sought out: the look of the land, the character of the children, the sandstone figures along the Wyoming border, and the sunsets, the roll of the prairie, the look of an old house . . . If I had not taken these photographs in 1936, and implanted them on my mind, studying them often when I was miles away from Colorado, I would never have written the novel. It was the persistence of these images that kept the ideas vital."

Michener's enquiring mind had led him to a general knowledge of the area's natural and man-made history, but it was Floyd Merrill who aroused his interest in two of eastern Colorado's more elusive facets: the mysteries of irrigation in the Platte river lands and the historical significance of Indian tribes whose hunting domain those lands had once been.

Merrill urged Michener over and over again to read the best book ever written about the American Indian, *The Delight Makers,* by a Swiss immigrant named Adolph Francis Alphonse Bandelier, and published at the end of the 19th century. "At that time I had no interest in Indians, and fended off his recommendation," Michener says. He finally read the book during his first visit to the cliff dwellings of Mesa Verde, and found it to be "a delicate, perceptive re-creation of an Indian culture . . . far ahead of its time in honestly evoking an Indian ambiance." Merrill had cast the hook that led to Michener's in-depth treatment of America's first inhabitants in *Centennial*.

While the story of the Indians appealed to him emotionally, the story of the Platte River intrigued the precise and scientific side of his nature. The most beneficial use of the Platte became a puzzle he found fascinating and challenging, and he took every opportunity to understand its intricacies. Again he remembers Merrill: "We examined every facet of the South Platte river system, the dams, the irrigation ditches . . . From him I learned what a river really was: a natural canal which could be used by clever men to move water where and when they wished."

On April 9, 1970, two days after Michener began his first notebook for *Centennial*, he listed on the the opening page, under a heading called "The Big Chunks," the subject matter for twelve chapers:

     1. Land
     2. Occupants
     3. Old Beaver
     4. Fort Brill
     5. The Wagon
     6. The Massacre — Buffalo
     7. The Cowboy
     8. The Smell of Sheep
     9. The Railroad
    10. The Lamberts
    11. Sugar Beets
    12. The Depression

Under a separate heading "The People," he listed proposed names for some of his main characters — John Brill, Levi Yoder, Capt. Schermerhorn, Lame Beaver, Willie Peters, Paul Chapman, Tim Calendar, Hung Wo, Paul and Martha Lambert, and Marquez. Of that page Michener says: "With very few changes, the original outline of twelve chapters withstood all kinds of challenges and alterations. Obviously, an opening chapter was added, and a closing. . . . Names did not survive so well. Of the originals, only Lame Beaver, the last part of Calendar and Marquez lasted. The vitality of the original idea, however, sketched out that first day, was remarkable."

While an idea is taking shape in Michener's mind he keeps it very much to himself. He dislikes making known his plans at an early date, and will often still be evasive long after he is firmly committed to a new project. Even late in the actual writing of *Centennial* he would answer an enquiry as to why he was in Colorado, by saying simply, "I'm looking into the possibility of doing some writing on the area," at a stage when he already had 80,000 words under his belt!

Once he had become fascinated by the possibilities of a western novel, Michener decided to revisit his old haunts, something he had not done for many years. Floyd Merrill had continued his correspondence and had repeatedly pressed him to turn his attention to a book centered on his Colorado experiences. On May 10, 1970, he wrote Merrill: "My wife and I are coming to Colorado to do a little exploring regarding some writing I may want to do. We expect to be in Greeley sometime around Tuesday, May 27. We are interested in much of Colorado history and wonder if you have from the schools a good history of the state that we could purchase? We are also much interested in a history of Weld County, any account of buffalo, beaver, Herefords, sheep and Folsom man . . ."

Michener's dusk shot of an avocet, barely distinguishable in the center foreground of this 1937 Colorado prairie scene, was image enough to remind him of his favorite western bird. In Chapter 9, *The Hunters*, he attributes to Jim Lloyd his own affection for this fragile creature: *On one of the islands, Jim found the bird which, even more than the soaring hawk, would epitomize for him this strange new land. It was a frail thing, walking delicately through marshes on slim yellow legs . . . Jim had never seen a bird like this and he laughed with pleasure as it tiptoed along the shore of the river, dipping its curved beak into wormholes.*

Elk browsing in the evening shadows of a mountain meadow, photographed by Michener forty years ago. Despite all the efforts at wildlife conservation during the intervening years, including the wise stewardship of the National Parks, it would be virtually impossible to record a similar scene today from a roadside viewpoint, except perhaps in the depth of winter when the press of summer and fall visitors has gone.

And to the superintendent of Fort Laramie National Monument in Wyoming he wrote: "My interests are rather general at this time, but I am concerned to know what Indians inhabited the area between the two Plattes, where the beavers lived in this area, where the buffalo flourished, and of course the general details of exploration and trail movement up to the building of the railroads. I could be much more specific but I am in that condition in which I don't know what I am looking for until I find it!"

Jim and Mari Michener left their home in Bucks County, Pennsylvania, on May 17, and drove to Sterling, Colorado, as the main base of their reconnaissance of the western plains. The trip occupied several weeks and gave Michener an opportunity to talk with experts in ranching, homesteading, farming, and that old tantalizer, the problems of irrigation. Many of these experts were introduced to him by a new-found friend in Sterling, Otto Unfug, a man of immense experience who had engaged in all kinds of occupations in the west, from rancher, cattle trader, newspaper editor, museum sponsor, real estate operator, to patron of the arts and amateur archeologist.

Unfug was a marvel. He brought to Michener sixteen men who had built irrigation ditches, seven old homesteaders, a dozen farmers. Whatever area Michener's fertile mind ranged over, 70-year-old Otto Unfug could find knowledgeable men and women to fill in the details. Of Unfug, he states: "He took me on a field trip to an abandoned line camp, one of those informal stations in the midst of nowhere, used by cowboys as overnight stops in the days when ranches ran for a hundred miles in any direction. I can never forget the beauty of that desolate station: a big stone barn whose century-old woodwork interior was as lovely as a Breughel painting, a small, low-slung stone farmhouse which nestled properly into its landscape. This camp was the kind of image a writer looks for, and when he sees it once, he holds on to it forever."

Michener was able, also, to spend several days with Floyd Merrill, "an old man now, hard hit by various attacks, but his wit was as sharp as ever. We went to see the incredible Big Thompson Diversion, which he had championed for so long, and saw the clear, cold water rushing out from beneath the mountains. We went onto the prairie to see the flowers — millions of them, though the casual eye might see nothing but sere grass — and then to his study, where hundreds of books I had not seen before bespoke his continuing interests. 'I'm thinking about that novel,' I told him. He nodded, and one week later he was dead."

Michener came home from the exploratory trip with all his old love for the lands between the Plattes rekindled, satisfied that the basic design for his western novel was sound, but knowing that it would probably require a further two years of intensive research. He dug in and turned to book after book to give him the background knowledge he needed for a story that would stretch from Lancaster, Pennsylvania, to the Continental Divide, from Chihuahua, Mexico, to north-west Wyoming.

Over the months he culled some three hundred books for background material to give him confidence in his subject. He would do final pinpoint research when he moved out west to begin writing, but the months of reading while he was still in Pennsylvania gave him a knowledgeable base from which he could begin to refine his specific interests later.

By July 4, a workday like any other, Michener had read enough on his subject to be able to request the following detailed information from J. Merrill Mattes, a noted authority on the Platte:

*Dear Dr. Mattes,*

*I have been working for some time on a projected novel covering the establishment and settlement of a small town on the left bank of the South Platte well west of Julesburg. Naturally, I have studied with considerable care your fine volume on the North Platte and am now prepared to ask you a few questions whose answers will be simple to you but somewhat obscure to me. If you could jot down the dates I would appreciate it very much.*

*1. I plan to use as my fictional base for this part of the story a Pennsylvania German leaving Pennsylvania and emigrating through either Independence or St. Joseph. My story would be easier for me to correlate if the trip took place sometime around 1838 but well before the gold rush of 1849–50. Would a solitary traveler from the east in 1838 join up with a group in Missouri before kicking off? What would be their logical destination, California or Oregon? (Obviously, my traveler is derailed and winds up in Colorado.) What are the best published sources for this early period?*

*2. When was the Court House named, not necessarily in print?*

*3. What was the earliest appearance of cholera? What was the earliest epidemic?*

*4. When was the elephant first discussed at camp fires?*

*5. When was the first mammoth excavated, in part or whole, in the Nebraska region?*

*6. When was the earliest covered wagon caravan along the South Platte?*

*7. I have studied your book carefully, but have perhaps missed a key section. What was the desirable time table for the trip west? Earliest kick off from Missouri? Typical halt at Fort Kearny? Typical passage of Scott's Bluffs? Latest safe passage of Fort Laramie? I note your statement on page 496: passage of Fort Laramie on July 5 seemed late. Do you happen to know when the Donner party left Laramie?*

*8. I was much fascinated by the recurrent phrase of travelers in Nebraska that it was different from the States, etc. At what point did your journalists, in general, think that they were leaving the States?*

*Your book is a remarkable repository of which you must feel proud. I noticed only one phenomenon, which struck me quite boldly, about which you do not pause for comment. Early in the reading I was impressed with the wide range of references used by the journalists for making comparisons. Then, on pages 422–425 came that splendid selection of descriptions of Scott's Bluffs, and I found these sometimes illiterate men thinking back on Gibraltar, Switzerland, the Alhambra, Heidelberg, Babylon, Nineveh, Thebes, Arabia, China, Rome, Athens, Bagdad and Stirling Castle. What really stunned me, however, was to find one writer comparing it to Petra! I was at Petra some years ago, and to get there was a major operation. It is incredible to think that these emigrants, back on the east coast of the United States, had already heard of the place and evaluated its quality. They were certainly not parochial.*

*I have asked too many questions, but you probably have all the answers at your finger tips. I would appreciate any guidance you could give me,*

*Most warmly,*
*James A. Michener*

Michener photographed this Colorado ranch scene in the late 1930's. This is the land to which the cowboys brought the longhorns from Texas in 1868; and here is the Hereford breed he selected to introduce from England to upgrade the herd on the Venneford cattle empire that sprawled for a hundred and fifty miles along the Colorado/Wyoming border.

Broken fences and drifting dust were the epitaph for dryland farmers of the dustbowl years. This early Michener photograph is one of the images of the Great Depression that were to shape his writing of the *Drylands* chapter of *Centennial* four decades later. *Fences were especially vulnerable. The terrible force would send a horde of tumbleweeds across a field; they would be imprisoned by some fence, and when the next storm hit, the weeds would catch so much dust that the fences would vanish and cattle would roam for a score of miles.*—Chapter 13, *Drylands*

This morning I woke up with a complete novel outlined. I had not thought of its subject since 1937, but now it stood forth in complete detail.

background, I suppose, is that many people have been after me to write about the United States, Helen Strauss and Hobart Lewis among my immediate friends, scores of my correspondents.

Also, the Centennial Commission has been having some private meetings with me on the subject of our natio two hundredth birthday, and I've been por ng over the secret report to the President, helping to draft certain sections.

The word Centennial must have remin ded me of the Centennial State, and of an imaginary plains town of that name which has lived with me since 1937 when I first saw the Platte, nighty and grubby river.

*I A*

1. Land
2. Animals
3. Old Beaver
4. Hurd-Hart- Fort Brill

---

Wagon-Yoder
Massacre- Schermehorn
Scarketts- Grandmother
Depression
Railroad- Hung Wo Fat
Winter- Chapman
Cowboy- Miller
Gold- ?
Sugarbeet- Marquez
Lambert- Grandmother
The Article
Buffalo- Barger

---

Centennial

Paul Yoder
John Brill
Scarketts
Hung Wo Fat          Calendar
Chapman              Garrett
Marquez
? Barger
Beaver
Lambert

---

THE PEOPLE

4. JOHN BRILL

5. LEVI YODER

6. CAPT. SCHERMERHORN - LAME BEAVE

7. WILLIE PETERS

8. PAUL CHAPMAN   GARRETT   TOM CALENDAR

9. HUNG WO

PAUL + MARTHA LAMBERT

1.    MARQUEZ

---

The Big Chunks

1. Land - POISON SPRING

2. Occupants

3. Old Beaver

4. FORT BRILL

5. The Wagon

6. the Massacre - BUFFALO

7. the Cowboy

8. the Sheep

9. the Railroad

10. the Scarketts LAMBERTS

11. SUGARBEETS

12. THE DEPRESSION

G.
L.

In every weather, the South Platte fascinated him. (Photo © Tessa Dalton)

The opening page of the first of many notebooks
Michener filled during the writing of *Centennial*.

The feedlot beside a sugar beet factory became part of the agricultural story in *Centennial*. Though Michener took this photograph in 1937, the scene today is still the same; unlike his early shot of downtown Denver, which has changed from a glorified cowtown to a sophisticated metropolis during the same period of time.

This pure American Gothic photograph suggests a little boy, like Timmy Grebe in *Centennial*, grown prematurely old under the strain of the Depression years. The homestead scene below, with its background of billowing cloud and hint of Springtime in the meadow's wildflowers, was typical of hundreds like it slowly decaying all across the Colorado plains in the late 1930's when Michener took these two shots.

After he returned from his first trip of May, 1970, Michener was not able, despite his excitement for his Colorado project, to give it his exclusive attention. He was not able to close his study door and take the phone off the hook, for as always there were a hundred people clamoring for his attention, quite apart from his own unabated interest in all that was going on around him. Michener could never shut himself off from the world. He's there in the mainstream of what's going on, politically, spiritually, morally — everywhere. His time is sought, his views are sought, his words are sought, and whenever it is for some cause or happening that interests him strongly, he becomes involved, with his time, his typewriter, or his presence.

In the spring of 1970 the campus killing at Kent State University concerned him deeply. There were so many conflicting principles at stake, and so much rhetoric and fog screening the vital issues involved that he took on the task of making a complete, book-length, investigative report that was published in 1971. To help him prepare his account, needed at breakneck speed for the presses, he was given the on-campus help, for a 2–3 month span, of a bright young *Digest* researcher, Leslie Laird, just graduated from college, as a liaison between him and the student faction. Leslie, as bright as a whole card of buttons, later joined us for two brief periods during the preparation of *Centennial*.

The Kent State diversion was typical of Michener. Sudden involvement can change his best-laid plans. It happened with *The Bridge at Andau*, his account of the Hungarian uprising, it happened with *Kent State*, it led to one of the most important articles of his career, written for the *New York Times* at the height of Watergate, and it will surely happen again. Understandably, for though most of Michener's works are written as fiction, his themes, however historically they may roam, are invariably linked with the ongoing condition of man.

In the instance of *Centennial*, the Kent State diversion slowed his preparation, and it was not until August 1972 that he felt sufficiently informed on the Platte and all its implications to plan his move to Denver for the actual writing of the novel. By that time he had already returned to the west many times by car, on one research subject alone covering the Oregon Trail route from St. Joseph, Missouri, to South Pass, Wyoming, mile by mile four times to help him understand the physical and psychological implications of that momentous journey. He also scoured the Lancaster area of Pennsylvania time and again, haunting the libraries and historical associations across the State in search of the substance that shaped the lives of Levi and Elly Zendt.

His first notebook was filled with minuscule handwritten notes of the contents for each of the twelve chapters he intended. Names, dates, maps of geologic strata, three different recipes for souse, information on wagons, guns, Indians, sheepmen, some notation on nearly every component that went into the final book. The handwriting is almost impossible to read, tiny and cramped. Michener has a great retentive memory, in this instance absolutely vital, for I doubt that even he was later able to decipher that wild hodge-podge of entries.

In September, Jim and Mari Michener headed west by car once more over the Oregon Trail route, to Denver, where Michener set up shop in a high-rise apartment within walking distance of the Denver Public Library — a most important prerequisite, for between October and December alone he read more than 100 titles in its Western History Room, ranging from *The World of the Prairie Dog* to *Irrigated Soils, Their Fertility and Management*. To Michener a library is the next best place to home, a haven of intellectual comfort. He is a connoisseur of libraries world-wide, and he rates the Denver Public Library as one of the finest in his travels.

Coupled with his reading, Michener immediately resumed his field trips. A few days after his arrival in Denver he drove with Dr. Lauren Wright, a professor of geology at Penn State University, to the solitary buttes east of Greeley which he planned to use in his novel. "After he had told me about the buttes, we stopped at the nearby ghost town of Keota, Colorado. I had known this town in its good days, when men and women of hope lived here in the belief that they could make the barren wastes of the American desert bloom. Once, years ago, I had spoken in the Keota school, whose broken windows and door ajar told the story of the vanished town. The railway station was torn down, the bank was level with the ground, save for the little concrete cube in which the iron vault was once hidden; the grain elevator was gone, and so was the fine wooden hotel.

Entry, actual size, in a Michener notebook. Never one to waste space, such notes were, on later consultation, often unreadable even by Michener himself. Usually, however, the mere act of making a notation was enough for it to remain in his memory.

"Only one thing still functioned, the ancient post office, and as Dr. Wright and I pushed open the creaking door the bell jangled, as it had been doing for half a century. A wispy old man stepped forward to greet us, unusually bright of eye and witty of speech."

His name was Clyde Stanley, and during a lifetime spent in Keota he had been homesteader, editor of the town newspaper, Land Commissioner and Postmaster. He had an amazingly clear memory of the old days and, like Floyd Merrill and Otto Unfug, he became a valued advisor for Michener on life in the area before, during and after the Great Depression.

Now settled in Denver, Michener could give his undivided attention to his novel. He knew without any further shade of doubt that he was going to turn his idea of April 7, 1970, into reality. It had taken him two and a half years of preliminary planning, and 35 years of nurturing his western memories while working in faraway corners of the world, to reach this point.

Chihuahua, Mexico, when Michener first went there some years before World War II. He told me that, of all foreign countries where he has lived, he probably knows Mexico best; and that he should have written a book about this land which held a very strong affection for him long before he came to tell the story of Tranquilino Marquez in *Centennial*. In the surrounding countryside he came upon the bucolic scene of the two young sheepherders with their flock; and in New Mexico found the shy Navajo shepherdess whose working dress confirms the earlier period of these photographs. Jim Michener took them all in the late 1930's.

# CHAPTER II

# THE LONG JOURNEYS

arly in January 1973 I joined Michener in Denver, after Tessa Dalton and I had completed our research in Pennsylvania on the 1844 wagon route Elly and Levi Zendt would take from Lancaster, Pennsylvania, on the first stage of their westward trek. When Michener sent us east we had no idea how much research he had himself done on that portion of his story — which is no doubt what he intended, so that we would go over the ground thoroughly from an absolutely cold start.

To uncover details of life in and around Lancaster in the mid-1840's, we hunted through the records of museums, libraries, historical societies and private collections. Surprisingly, we came across a greater number of personal accounts of Pennsylvania life in the mid-1700's than we did for the mid-1800's, largely I suspect because the pattern of rural and town existence had already become standardized and predictable by the mid-19th century — and it seemed no more necessary to record than an account of travelling on the Pennsylvania Turnpike would be to a motorist today. But the routes to the west, the fortunes of wagoners, and accounts of flatboat journeys down the Ohio River had been documented sufficiently for us to collect the components for Elly and Levi's travels. Population counts, weather records, spelling of place names, sizes of farms, costs of tolls, details of wagon building, and a hundred other supportive facts that would give us the feel of the times were unearthed, though many of them, of course, would never appear in the book.

Our Pennsylvania journey brought that part of Michener's story very much alive, and triggered a curiosity to find out all we could on his other chapters. When we talked about the Zendt passage west, on our return to Denver, Michener pooled his own findings and we discussed the fortunes of Levi and Elly as though we were personally responsible for the success of their journey. What would have been the condition of the Susquehanna River at the time they crossed the covered Columbia Bridge to the west bank in February? Would they have taken the old grade road over the Alleghenies, or the faster but steeper Forbes Road, at a time of year when snowstorms could still be a threat? Where would it be safe for them to ford the Juniata River? At which inns along the route might they stop? By the time we had the runaway pair safely on their flatboat to Cairo, Illinois, a sinkhole where we knew they would find trouble, we felt so much a part of their trials that we could have been in the wagon with them.

A few days later we were in our own wagon, this time Michener's white Chevrolet, heading south out of Denver for Texas, to throw together a bunch of longhorns we would somehow succeed in driving back up to the Wyoming border. Michener's instructions had been precise. We should join him at his apartment at 6:00 a.m., on Friday, January 19, and be prepared to stay away about a week. There would only be the three of us for this field trip — Mari had to return to tidy up domestic details back east in Bucks County.

Before we left, Mari took me aside, and in whispered tones gave strict instructions as to how I should watch over "Mich" — as she calls him. To my still-present anxiety and nervousness about whether I could measure up to Michener's exacting standards, she now added a new layer of concern, explaining that he had suffered a serious heart attack some years earlier and needed lots of rest, particularly in the afternoons. It was my responsibility to see that he had a nap and that we did not drive too far on any one day. She then gave me specific instructions as to what I should do if he suffered a relapse. I now felt doubly agitated, and after a restless night, in which I imagined every possible combination of exigencies that might assail us on the journey, awoke at 4:00 a.m. on the day of our departure.

In a frigid Colorado dawn, with around six inches of snow already packed hard in the streets and more expected hourly, we reached Michener's apartment at 6:00 a.m. to find him already settled in the front passenger seat of the car, huddled down in a thick coat, a black quilted cap pulled low over his forehead, peering with great concentration at a map of Texas. We piled in our gear and took off. I drove through the deserted downtown area, eased the car onto Interstate 25 South and was into the first hour of a journey I faced with considerable apprehension. Michener continued the surveillance of his maps, pausing repeatedly to gaze at the bastion front range of the Rockies to our right, and to give us snippets of information on their history, particularly on Pikes Peak, disappointing visually in its role as Colorado's highest mountain but fascinating in its context of the gold rush days.

I drove 220 miles, a lot of it through light snow, before we stopped for breakfast in a roadside café at Raton, New Mexico, a pivotal point where we would swing southeast into the Texas Panhandle. With some pride and relief that we had come thus far without incident, I looked forward to a leisurely breakfast. But it was not to be. Michener ordered a glass of buttermilk and a pancake, bought two newspapers to bring him up-to-date on local and national news, and had finished his breakfast and was up and moving before my eggs had even touched the table. With some hesitancy I asked if it would be all right for us to eat our meal. "Of course," he said, "I'll wait in the car."

When he has finished a meal Michener is immediately ready to move on, to get back to work, and he can be oblivious of those around him. Many people have taken his abrupt departures from luncheon and dinner tables as evidence of some displeasure. Rarely is this so. He merely does not want to waste time; for him there is no more precious commodity, because he can accomplish so much with it. To squander it on small talk is a negation he cannot bear.

We continued on our journey, picked up the makings of a frugal lunch — including two of Michener's favorites, cookies and jellybeans — and stopped beside a tributary of the Canadian River. If Michener has two overriding interests on a journey, they are maps and rivers. At every gas stop we picked up more maps, and the finer points of difference between competing oil companies' free maps were apparent to him within minutes. He can look at a map and virtually see in his mind the countryside it covers. For want of a new word, Michener is a totally addicted mapaholic.

The Susquehanna River at Columbia, Pennsylvania. In *Centennial*, Levi and Elly Zendt crossed here over the world's longest covered bridge. *It was only twelve miles to Columbia, where the famous bridge waited to lift them across the mighty Susquehanna . . . And they entered upon the very long covered bridge, with its two separated tracks plus a third for persons walking their horses . . .*—Chapter 6, *The Wagon and the Elephant*

COLUMBIA

Originally Wright's Ferry, founded by John Wright in 1726. An early center for turnpike, canal, and railroad activity, at an important Susquehanna River crossing. First bridge built in 1812.

PENNSYLVANIA HISTORICAL AND MUSEUM COMMISSION

Four miles west of Bedford, Pennsylvania, the *Old Forks Inn* still stands at the junction of routes 30 and 31, formerly named the Forbes Road and Glade Road, two competing turnpikes that crossed the Alleghenies to Pittsburgh. Levi and Elly Zendt took the left fork, the longer but easier Glade Road, for their assault of the mountains, at a time, 1844, when inns such as this were situated almost every mile to help travelers on their way.

And when he reaches a river he is compelled to walk its banks. He feels rivers as others feel the lure of mountains. They speak to him of life for man and nature, and he ponders their complexities, their potential, their shortcomings. For him the most fascinating of America's rivers is the mighty Colorado, and he confessed that if he were younger he would like nothing more than to write a book devoted exclusively to the natural and historic phenomena of that magnificent river.

Finally, that first day of our field trip, having covered nearly 600 miles during which he allowed himself not so much as a yawn, let alone a nap, we pulled into Canyon, west Texas. I asked whether he would like me to find a Holiday Inn, or something of that nature. "No. Let's look for something quiet on the edge of town," he said. I drove until we stopped at a clean, eight-dollar a night, totally unpretentious motor court where Canyon begins to fade again into the Texas plains. Within seconds I understood why he had chosen it. He had spotted a practice basketball net in the forecourt. "Hey, John, let's shoot a few baskets. Ask them in the office if they've got a ball we could borrow," he suggested after I had registered.

He bounced that ball around as though he were warming up for a tournament game, leaving me flatfooted. I knew he had gone to college in Pennsylvania on a basketball scholarship — and at 66 years of age he was still no slouch at the hoop. Next he suggested that we walk to our venue for 8:00 a.m. the next morning, the Panhandle Plains Museum of West Texas University. And to end that first day he said he'd skip dinner because he had two or three hours' reading he wanted to finish! I went to bed more concerned about my health than his.

The Panhandle Plains Museum tells the story of the cattleman and the cowboy simply and eloquently, and there we were able to study the rigging of ancient saddles, the construction of a chuck wagon, the clothing and equipment of a trailhand more than a hundred years ago, how to make good sourdough biscuits, the sidearms a cowboy would have carried, just about everything we needed to know to equip our outfit for their journey. On that trip, and on several more later in the year, we visited other museums from Texas to Montana in our search for authenticity on the old-time cowboy, but nowhere could match the solid presentation of facts we found under the guidance of C. Boone McLure at the Panhandle Plains Museum in Canyon, Texas.

While Tessa Dalton was busy photographing saddles, stirrups, bedrolls, and cook's preferred victuals for the chuck wagon, Jim Michener made notes in a small spiral-bound, 3 x 4½-inch notebook. He never went anywhere without one of these. Sometimes he would jot down only a couple of words to remind him of a mass of information he had just absorbed; another time it might be a list of 20 possible first and last names for one of his characters.

The name game absorbed many miles of our travels. We would each contribute suggestions until he decided on those that best suited the character he had in mind. He had, for example, a lot of trouble until he hit on the simple combination of Jim and Lloyd for the 14-year-old Texas lad who would later run the Venneford ranch. The combination of Charlotte and Buckland, for the well-bred though not high-society English girl Lloyd later married, was almost as difficult, and Michener discarded a host of alternatives along the way. Georgina Tredinnick, Harriet Armitage, and Jane Pollard all bowed to Charlotte Buckland as his final choice for the high-spirited yet stubborn girl who would later rule Venneford Castle like a true chatelaine. There are around 70 main characters in *Centennial*, and to find names that sounded appropriate for the parts they played, as well as being in keeping with their family origins and their time in history, was an important and pleasurable part of our research, rather like a game of literary Scrabble.

In these long discussions on names we would also argue over what the characters in question would believe, do and say. His or her history was crucial and his or her philosophy was always analyzed most critically. We would gradually shape Poteet, Skimmerhorn, Charlotte, and the whole cast, until we knew the patterns of their behaviour as well as we would know those of close friends.

Our research in Texas took us briefly to the Cowboy Hall of Fame, in Oklahoma City, then to the 6666 Ranch at Guthrie, one of the famous old spreads of the west, where we gained information on the terrain, vegetation and weather our own herd would encounter during its journey. Next we went to Jacksboro, an old town built around a square, where Poteet would recruit cowboys for his cattle drive. Hitching posts had long since given way to parking meters, but the cocky, pimply youths, handling their pickups with as much swagger as though they had just ridden into town astride snorting, prancing stallions, were still in essence the same confident, muscle-flexing youths who volunteered for the trail north.

As we crossed the countryside Tessa kept notes on the terrain the cattle would encounter on their way toward Horsehead Crossing on the Pecos River. "From Jacksboro — slight hills covered with mesquite grass and scrub oak — many water holes — much cactus — hilly outcroppings on right — flatter on left — opens up just before narrowing into Bryson. Mistletoe on trees. Gently undulating country — live oaks. Flatter country around Graham — opening up at Eddelman Lake. Slight climb — undulating. Left in New Castle. Over Brazos River — open at sides — forward views limited — ridged hills — undulating road climbing slowly — generally flatter vistas. Four miles past Brazos — wide-open vista on left. Memorial plaque for three 15-year-old boys killed by Comanches in Elm Creek raid, July 17, 1867." And so on, for mile after mile she recorded the scene, stopping for photographs frequently. And at the end of this section of her Texas notes she added, "Check animals, birds, trees, etc., on trail."

Early one morning, after our usual pre-breakfast drive, we stopped at a less than modest café on the outskirts of Robert Lee, a small town poised at the edge of the Llano Estacado, the still-forbidding terrain that broke the fortunes of many cattlemen who attempted to coax herds across it in the heydays of the great cattle drives. We pushed open the door of the café and I knew at once that we were in the kind of surroundings that Michener loves. The men who, obviously, ran the town sat at one of the oilcloth-covered tables, sipping black coffee from thick-lipped mugs. The group included an unkempt, obese law officer strung about with weaponry like Hemingway going on safari, a reedy-voiced emaciate who could have been the judge, a noisy, shiny-suited character in high boots who might have been the mayor, and one or two other stubble-jawed heroes. They looked at us with evident suspicion. We were unwelcome strangers, whatever we were at.

Michener went to a nearby table and asked for his usual glass of buttermilk. Tessa asked for an omelette, only to be informed that the cook had never been asked to make one before, but that he would try. She settled, as I did, for pancakes, selected from a grease-stained menu that looked as though it had been handed down from father to son. I could sense that Jim was eager to draw this attractive group into conversation, and only our imminent, prearranged appointment with the town's historian prevented him. With a sigh he got up and left. If Michener were offered a choice between lunch at the "21" Club in New York or breakfast at that inspirational café, he would choose a meal at Robert Lee, Texas, every time.

Before he left Pennsylvania, Michener had researched the authentic old cowboy

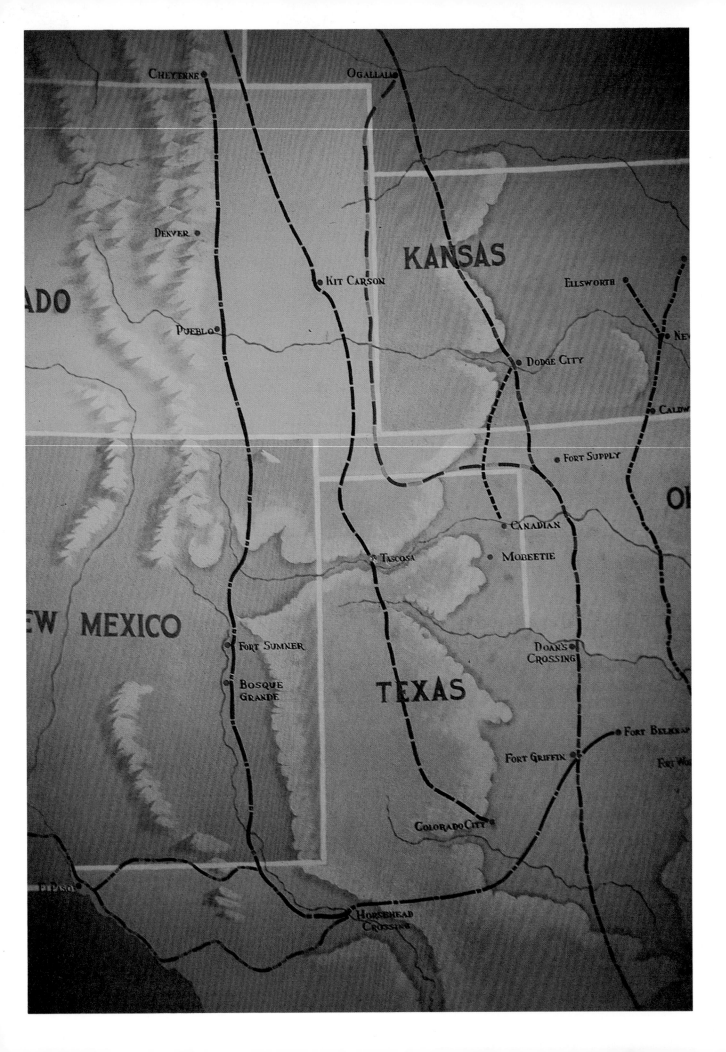

Map showing the long south-western loop of the Goodnight-Loving cattle trail across the *Llano Estacado* to Horsehead Crossing, where it turned northward up the Pecos River toward Colorado and Cheyenne.

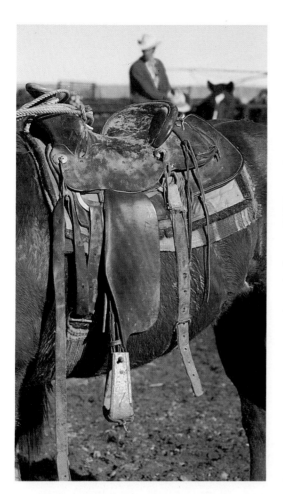

At the Panhandle Plains Museum, Canyon, west Texas, we researched equipment used in the everyday life of the trail-herd cowboy. Apart from his saddle *. . . No item was more important than the chuckwagon. From the front it looked like any standard, long-bedded, canvas-covered prairie wagon, except that from its sides hung suspended an unusual array of pans, buckets, axes and canvas bags.*—Chapter 8, *The Cowboys*—(Photo © Tessa Dalton)

From his travelling kitchen Nacho produced the food that sustained the cowboys through drought, storm·and attack. *To make his biscuits he took from the crock a good helping of sourdough, mixed it with flour, water and salt, and pinched off nubbins, which he placed around the bottom of a dutch oven . . . Nacho's biscuits were the best the men had ever eaten . . . brown and crisp on top, well done on the bottom, and just about perfect inside.*—Chapter 8, *The Cowboys*

songs, and had taped them as a musical background for our own Chevy wagon trail through Texas. As we drove he would click in a cassette and the strains of *Red River Valley, I Ride an Old Paint,* the great lyrics of *Strawberry Roan,* and the words and music of a dozen more ballads added to the feeling that we were almost within shouting distance of the men we had recruited to throw our bunch of cattle together. Over and over we played those songs, south-west to Horsehead Crossing, up the Pecos River, through New Mexico north to Colorado.

We reached famed Horsehead Crossing on the Pecos River just as the sun was going down on Wednesday, January 24, five days out of Denver and at the southern-most point of our cattle trail. The glinting rays of the evening sun reflecting from the ditch they call the Pecos emphasized the life-saving reward its brackish waters offered to parched and exhausted men and cattle alike when they reached the end of that desperate leg of their journey across the Llano Estacado.

Michener scooped up a mouthful of the Pecos, tasted its salty tang, and wisely spat it back into the stream. "I'd hate to cross a hundred miles of desert just for that," he said. "It makes me want to send our cattle up a different trail!"

Once we had decided on Venneford as the name of the English earl who would colonize a northern Colorado cattle ranch from horizon to horizon, we had to decide on the brand that Poteet and his men would burn into the hides of the long-horns before they moved out of Texas on the Goodnight-Loving trail. We finally agreed on the Crown Vee, a simple one-iron brand that would delight the heart of the most fastidious cattleman. It was especially appropriate that the two-eared crown with the V suggested the simple facial outline of a steer. We toyed with several possible alternative designs for the brand, including the two shown in the margin, but finally settled on the simple Crown Vee that became famous through-out the west. I was very proud of my design. On one of our frequent visits to Cheyenne, I submitted it for approval as an actual, legitimate 1973 brand, more in hope than expectation, however, for all the simple designs for brands have long since been registered. I took it as a good omen when I learned that such a combina-tion had never, in fact, been recorded for Laramie County, the area of Wyoming into which the Venneford ranch strayed from its Colorado confines. The brand is now registered with the Wyoming Livestock Commission, in the name of James A. Michener, and he could run his own Crown Vee cattle in Laramie County anytime the urge to be a rancher proves too strong to resist.

Crown Vee

At Horsehead Crossing we turned north for our return journey, on the way choosing Las Vegas, New Mexico, as an appropriate town in which our cowboys might pause to remind themselves of the good things of life they had forsworn since leaving Jacksboro. Our other concern was to scout the rivers that 2,700 long-horns would have to cross on the trail north — a northern reach of the Pecos, the Purgatoire, the Arkansas, and finally the South Platte itself. We returned to Denver to the strains of *Roll on Little Dogies, Roll On,* satisfied that we had a good chance of getting our cattle successfully up the trail Michener had chosen. The foray into Texas had been a rewarding trip. I had forgotten all about trying to force afternoon naps on him — it would have been impossible, anyway, to do so against his will — and I had learned that I was working, contrary to all the rumors I had heard, for a man of some warmth and wit in addition to his hard-driving disciplines as a writer. He wrote that it was one of the best field trips he had ever taken.

Our next distant sortie took us two hundred miles into Mexico, to Chihuahua, Pancho Villa's stronghold and the provincial capital of an area Michener chose as the home of his Colorado migrant beet worker, Tranquilino Marquez. In Chihuahua we talked with Francisco Almeda, an aged history professor who cautiously opened his door inch by inch in response to Jim's peremptory knock, but who helped us considerably with a fund of information on the old days of strife and terror in the region. Of our enquiry as to whether we should talk with Pancho Villa's widow, he replied: "You can talk with them, for there are many who claim that title, but you must remember that legend has long since corrupted the truth of memory." We did not seek out his widow, but we did go to a scene of incontrovertible truth, the crossroads in Chihuahua at which Villa was finally ambushed and killed.

Using Chihuahua as a base, we drove westward one morning to the old deserted silver-mining town of Cusihuiriachi, its abandoned houses strung haphazardly along a stream that wound between hills once loaded with silver. It had been a company town, Mexican-owned but run by American engineers and mined for pitiful wages by peasant labor. Cusi was now, to all intents, a ghost town. At one point a group of curious, bright-eyed children, offspring of the few remaining inhabitants, swarmed round Jim as he sat on a crumbling wall to contemplate the stream, the old church, and the dirt-surfaced main street that straggled up the valley. The children stood dutifully while we photographed them with Jim, but not until one sandy-haired cherub had had time to rush to the stream to wash her hands before posing for the shot. Was her fair complexion, I wondered, a link with those far-off days when *norteamericanos* gouged wealth from the mountains of the Sierra Madre?

We had reached Cusihuiriachi over an all but nonexistent rocky road that nearly tore the bottom out of the car, but we finally got out of the valley in one piece, and left behind the town whose setting and atmosphere contributed much to the town of Temchic in *Centennial*. We stayed only a few days in Mexico, but long enough for Michener to refresh his memory of an area he had formerly known well, and for him to capture the images he needed to bring to life the story of his Mexican family. In Aquiles Serdan, Michener studied a massive pair of church doors he describes in the book as belonging to the church at Santa Ynez, his fictional home of Tranquilino and Serafina Marquez; in Chihuahua again, he saw Tarahumare Indians of another generation than those he had photographed in the mid-30's, but they were still the same "slim, deerlike people" he remembered.

One afternoon we stopped by the roadside to watch a train of flatcars and boxcars about half a mile away across a valley, chuffing and clanking toward a cleft in the hills. The rolling stock was antique, the engine was a snorting, puffing billy that should have been put out to grass long ago, yet there it was chugging northward toward the border, as though time had stood still since the *revolución*. Only the rattle of machine-gun fire and the sight of running figures were missing from the scene, and it was not difficult to imagine them.

We left Mexico to music of the revolution and sad songs of love on another of Michener's tapes. One of his favorites, *La Adelita,* was missing from his collection, until Tessa found a recording of it in a Chihuahua music shop. For Michener it was undoubtedly the finest piece of research she did on that trip. On the way home we stopped in Santa Fe, then drove slowly through the lovely country north of Taos which had appealed so much to Tranquilino before he went to work in Potato Brumbaugh's beet fields. Our second long-distance field trip was over. Again, this time with Mari Michener to make up the full team and orchestrate Jim's rest periods much more successfully than I could ever have hoped, we returned to Denver with the material we needed, and with our amity intact.

Each time we returned to Denver it snowed some more, adding white on white day after day until the winter of 1972–73 went unmourned into the record books.

49

*. . . It was from the rear that it seemed so striking, for there a boxlike structure had been fastened in such a way that the back could be lowered and made into a stout table, supported by a folding leg. Behind this collapsible table, hidden from sight until it was dropped, nested seven neat drawers, each with a brass handle, each with a store of useful or delicious items.*—Chapter 8, *The Cowboys*

The long-distance field trips to Texas and Mexico gave us a chance to leave behind those boringly repetitive snowfalls in search of warmer climes, but on the next lengthy excursion a typical Wyoming spring blizzard made us pay for our brief times in the sun.

On April 6, Jim and Mari Michener, Tessa Dalton and I headed north out of Denver en route to Wyoming, Idaho and Montana. Our first call was at the University of Wyoming in Laramie to meet with Dr. George Frison, a world-renowned authority on ancient bison and the mammoth. George Frison, formerly a Wyoming rancher whose curiosity toward the fossil riches that lay literally at his feet led him to pursue a new career in archeology, showed Jim Michener physical evidence of paleo-Indian existence, and arranged for him a most exciting demonstration by a modern-day flint-knapper.

Michener recorded this fascinating item of research, and his account shows the extent to which he will burrow into a subject to ferret out a complete knowledge of it. A multiplication of this example, several hundred times in the course of his preparation of *Centennial,* gives some idea of extraordinary lengths to which he will go in his search for accuracy. But it also shows his deep love of learning for its own sake, of acquiring knowledge to enrich his experience of life, irrespective of its application to any work he may have in hand. If Michener meets a shoemender he will be fascinated by that man's skills. He is unable to resist finding out how things work. For Michener, living is learning, and his desire to acquire knowledge is almost aberrative in its intensity.

## CASE HISTORY OF A SEGMENT

*It might be interesting to see how an author works on a specific problem. I wanted to provide a faithful account of how the earliest man in Colorado worked in making a point for his spear. The first step would be to study all available documents before attempting to write, visit all museums, and study all kinds of reports, visiting the men in question if possible. The second would be to find someone living who was trying to make points in the old way. And after all this had been done, then write the segment. Because time was a factor, I decided to follow a course I had often followed before, and with good results. It's a pattern I advocate for all writers.*

*I would do all the study possible, reading every known thing on the subject that I could get my hands on, but while I was doing it I would draft the chapter, so that I would always have before me a structure on which I and others could work when the time came. This version would contain many errors, which did not concern me, but also a basic structure that was solid, sound and permanent. I now had something to work on.*

*In working through this material I came upon an excellent book, John E. Pfeiffer's* The Emergence of Man (1972), *and on page 407 I found his report of having worked with Donald Crabtree of Idaho, perhaps the world's most knowledgeable man in this field. I therefore wrote to Crabtree, asking if he would vet this short section, and I was not loath to do this because in my mail I get similar requests from all over the world. Indeed, while working in Denver I had received several.*

*Crabtree did a remarkable job. He not only sent me a very full letter, but he also worked over every line of the manuscript, adding comments that would later help much in revision. Crabtree objected to numerous points in my manuscript, pointing out especially the weaknesses in my theory of percussion as a means of making a Folsom point (that is, hammer striking a chisel). His criticisms were so cogent that no one could deny them.*

*In the meantime I had met, by sheerest accident, Marie Wormington, dean of American scholars regarding early man. Governor Love had asked me to serve on a commission identifying Colorado's more precious natural monuments, and Dr. Wormington was also on the panel. At a meeting later she informed me that a young man named Bruce Bradley, on leave from Cambridge University in England, happened to be in the west, and she arranged a meeting for us.*

*At this meeting Bradley, who is now one of the world's top flint-knappers, showed me how he made Folsom points, and it was a most incredible performance. Next day he was to give a fuller demonstration at the University of Wyoming, so I traveled there to watch him perform before a group of sixty admiring graduate students. That day we had a real blizzard and were immured for two days, during which Bradley read my manuscript and gave me many verbal comments; he confirmed many of Crabtree's criticisms, but most valuable were his actual demonstrations. Taking the verbal and tactile, I think I know how a point was made.*

*More important, perhaps, when Bradley returned to Cambridge he sent me a Folsom point he had made. But in the meantime Dr. Wormington had been giving me hell for writing about the Folsom point, because this meant that I had also to write about the bison. She very much wanted me to write about the Clovis point, which she liked better, because this would enable me to write also about the mammoth, a beast she loved. She was both argumentative and persuasive, and when she finally produced one of the most beautiful Clovis points ever made, she convinced me that it was real and basic, whereas the Folsom was rococo and ornamental. With all this and much more data, I then sat down to redraft my segment, and came up with a redraft which I passed along to Dr. Wormington, who made her own sage comments on it. After much re-working, the final came out, after editing by Erskine [Michener's Random House editor] and others.*

*In the meantime I was working in Lincoln, Nebraska, with two of the world's greatest authorities on Pleistocene and Recent mammals, Schultz and Stout, and they were encouraging me also to switch from the bison to the mammoth. So that when the final version was completed, it had been vetted by the man who knew most about flint-knapping, the young man who was the world's best in actually making flints, the woman who knew most about early man in America, and the two great scholars who led the field in animal studies. Their advice changed the chapter very much.*

*When I was finished I happened to be working with Gregg Scott on a water problem, and he chanced to say, "If you're interested in early man, you may be interested in this," and he showed me a perfectly wonderful Folsom point made by a man I had never heard of, and this man, under Scott's personal surveillance, was making his points in precisely the way I had deduced working a priori from such data as I had when I began.*

*This man did use the percussion method, he did wedge the flints rather than hold them in his palm, he did follow every one of my finishing procedures. I got in touch with him by phone to confirm for myself that he was doing it the way I had guessed, and he was duplicating my process entirely. When I told him of Crabtree's and Bradley's system, and of the fact that leading scholars in France and Russia support them, he merely said that he guessed that in the old days lots of men followed lots of different processes, and that Crabtree's might be a lot better for the average workman but that his was best for him. All I can say is that using the Centennial system as devised by that old flint-knapper Michener 12,000 years ago, he was coming up with some damned fine points.*

A fading sign on a Texas county road marks the turnoff to Horsehead Crossing, whose forlorn, forgotten banks we reached at sundown.

The *Llano Estacado. When the sun rose the men caught their first full impact of the Llano, for over the land before them they could see not one tree, nor any shrub of size, nor any trail marking, nor any sign of habitation. It was the most bleak and arid space they had ever surveyed, and it promised nothing.*—Chapter 8, *The Cowboys*

*Parallel with this other work, I was meeting with Marie Wormington at her home in Denver and she was propagandizing me, in the best sense of that term, to base my story on the Clovis point and the mammoth. She got nowhere in her argument until one day she said something which struck me as overwhelmingly appropriate. She said, "After all, the Clovis point is a Romanesque simplicity, while the Folsom is a Gothic adornment." I began to look at the points again and saw the soundness of her reasoning. I therefore gave her one of my versions to look at, and we went over the material together, line by line. Later I gave her my final version, and she hacked it up, and then she saw the last yellow-sheet version, and made the changes indicated on it. She also gave me an eight-step procedure which she advocated, and we reached some kind of compromise. I enjoyed her comments enormously.*

*In the meantime she had given me the draft of her new book, and I had read with great interest her reactions to the Calico site in California, and I revised both my copy and my notes to accommodate these findings. In this intricate manner, I devised the approach which resulted in the test as it appeared in the book. Then Kings and Erskine reviewed it for literary appropriateness, and I found that I could allow them to change hardly a word, since each phrase had its peculiar weight and meaning. At the end, I felt that I knew something about flint-knapping and I hope I relayed some of that response.*

We left Laramie after a two-day blizzard had played itself out and Interstate 80 was reopened to traffic. We made our way cautiously toward Rawlins and the western parts of Wyoming, threading past overturned and abandoned semi-trailers — eight of them together at one point, slewed in a grotesque pattern at the brow of a long hill — then turned northwest toward Jackson Hole and the Idaho site of the 1827 rendezvous of mountain men held at the southern end of Bear Lake.

Although we had already covered the story of the mountain men in great detail, Michener wanted to see for himself the actual known site of one of those hell-raising celebrations. Personal reconnaisance of sites he uses in his books is one of his hard and fast rules. Written accounts by others, photographs, hearsay may all add to his knowledge of a location, but he will not write his own scene until he has looked over an actual piece of terrain he intends to describe — whether the site is an historic reality, as in the case of Bear Lake, or part of the fictional background to his story. For the scene in *Centennial* where the cowboys' trail herd is attacked by the Kansas outlaws, we drove for two or more hours in the area of eastern Colorado where the bandits operated, before finding a lay of land that suited him. Leaving the car, he wandered several hundred yards into his scene, making a few notes, drawing a rough map in his notebook. Even his dinosaurs wallow in ponds he personally selected for their use.

After Bear Lake and a look at Jackson Hole, hub of the mountainous region of the beaver trappers, we crossed back into Idaho and drove up the west mountain flank to Yellowstone Park, whose wildlife in winter Michener wanted to see. Gone were the human hordes of summer that drive animals to the hinterlands of the park, and along the few roads in the northern section kept open throughout the year we saw at close quarters buffalo, bighorn sheep, elk, deer and moose. Only the bears were absent, still in hibernation. Yellowstone Park was no new ground to Michener, for he had visited and photographed it during his years in Greeley, but it was the first time any of us had seen it in its winter coat, and it was very impressive indeed. At times during our journeys of research we would make diversions to places Jim had seen in earlier years and wanted to visit again. Yellowstone was one such.

To reach the Big Horn country of Wyoming we now had to detour out of the north entrance to the park into Montana, before dropping down through the Crow Reservation and past the Custer Battlefield to Sheridan, Wyoming. Other more direct routes are closed in winter. We had come to this area to talk cattle ranching along those regions of the Powder River, east of Sheridan, opened up by the cattle barons of England and Scotland in the old days; and in Cody, to the west of the Big Horn range, where a large Simmenthal ranch could give us knowledge of a breed Jim would introduce in the last chapter of *Centennial* as part of the most recent experiments in cross-breeding. For four days we thought and talked cattle with a cross-section of cattlemen of all opinions, all of them hospitable and interested in Jim's efforts to find a viable new pattern of operation for the Venneford ranch along the Colorado/Wyoming border. Remarked one gnarled survivor of many more years of loss than profit: "If you take my advice you'll sell the whole outfit off to a developer. Only fools and gamblers go in for cattle ranching, and I can tell you're neither one of them!"

We returned to Denver on April 15, after a nine-day swing of more than 2,000 miles. We had dug a little deeper on early man, mountain men and cattlemen, and we returned from Cody through Shoshone and the Wind River Canyon, another delight to Jim, for the exposed strata of its walls are a complete geologic time clock from Pennsylvanian to Pre-Cambrian eras. We promised ourselves that when summer returned we would join George Frison on one of his archeologic digs and seek our own mammoth, and our own spear point.

A week after our return from Wyoming we were in Lincoln, Nebraska, with Dr. Bertrand Schultz and Professor Mylan Stout, of the University of Nebraska, following the trail of ancient Indians and animals, pursuing the cultures of the Folsom and Clovis points, and discussing the evidence that climatologists present to support their reasons for the disappearance of large mammals in the last Pleistocene extinction some 14,000 years ago. Working with these two eminent and kindly men was a great pleasure and led to a continuing friendship and exchange of ideas in the years following.

On leaving Lincoln, Jim let it be known that he intended to return to the University of Nebraska later in the year, not this time to ponder the fossil bones of ancient animals, but to watch the carnage of the annual football clash between the universities of Nebraska and Colorado, to which he alludes in *Centennial*'s final chapter. Bert Schultz was as delighted by Michener's interest in this latter-day bone-crunching ceremony as he was by his fascination with the killing sites of ancient days.

We drove back from Lincoln along the Platte, stopping frequently to view the unpredictably wandering course of the river that is the binding thread of Michener's book. He never tired of watching its muddy waters on their relentless eastward journey, giving life to parched plains and still beckoning to strong men and women as it had done through the centuries. Pasquinel and McKeag knew its moods and vagaries, the Pawnee, Arapaho and Sioux flourished and suffered from its quixotic nature, Levi Zendt and Elly urged their oxen toward its succoring protection. If ever there has been a river of history in the development of the western lands of America, it has been the Platte, disreputable and scruffy though it most often is. Michener loves its every strength and fault.

By May we were all beginning to feel that our efforts might produce a worthwhile story of the west. Jim began to confide that he was feeling optimistic about *Centennial,* as he had now firmly decided to call it. We were all more relaxed, there was a sense of achievement in the air, which, coupled with spring, made us all feel

Castle Gap, at the southern extremity of the *Llano Estacado,* close to Horehead Crossing in the foreground. *At the top of the pass, that strange cleft between hills so flat they might have been scraped across the top with a ruler, the cattle sensed that water lay below them in the distant valley, and they surged forward with new hope.*—Chapter 8, *The Cowboys*

Eighty miles across the arid *Llano Estacado* brought the parched Crown Vee cattle to this vital crossing of the Pecos River at the axis of the Goodnight-Loving Trail. *They surged into the stream past the skeleton horseheads and stood there for some minutes before drinking. Then, unlike the men who drank in foolish gulps, they took small sips, lowing as they did, until the whole muddy stream echoed with their joy.*—Chapter 8, *The Cowboys*—(Photo © Tessa Dalton)

*The Pecos was a preposterous river ... about eighteen feet across, as shallow as six inches in some parts, only a little deeper in others ... Jim Lloyd tried it, and it was brackish, tasting of alkali even at the good part. Farther up you couldn't keep the water in your mouth, let alone swallow it.*—Chapter 8, *The Cowboys*

buoyant. Leslie Laird, who had worked with Jim for a short period on the early chapter of Colorado's geology, before Tessa Dalton and I came on the scene, now joined us for a jaunt that was pure pleasure, a five-day sortie into western Colorado, northern Arizona and Utah.

At the time I could not quite understand the motive for the journey, but on reviewing Michener's early photographs of the 1930's some time after the publication of *Centennial,* I realized what it had all been about. Each place to which we went, the Grand Canyon, Zion National Park, Canyonlands and Bryce Canyon National Parks, to the superb scoured moonscapes of Glen Canyon National Recreation Area and the cliff dwellings of Mesa Verde, was for Jim a revival of old memories, of those times in the Depression years when he had ventured from the academic confines of Greeley to experience the extraordinary grandeur of the western states. On the way home through western Colorado, through Durango and Montrose, he merged recollection with the reality of the moment and made notes on the country that Paul Garrett would drive through on his environmental journeys.

On Saturday evening, May 26, we stopped for the night in Montrose, Colorado. At the end of a tiring drive, Jim had set his heart on a prime-rib dinner, and his day seemed complete when we sat down in a gaudy steakhouse with the Saturday night crowd and found that "Prime Rib, cattlemen's cut, *au jus*" was the featured special. In anticipation he even joined us in a drink, a rare indication of his beatific mood. Then suddenly his evening was completely spoiled. Our waitress informed us that the prime rib was off, and Jim subsided into a petulant depression from which none of us was able to rescue him. Neither the Alaska king crab, poetically described as "denizens of the deep," nor the alternatives of six other cuts of steak could mollify his sense of frustation. He sat, eyes down, now short-tempered where he had been happy and expansive, incapable of alternative.

It was childish and spoiled behaviour, and it pointed up the contradictory facets of the Michener temperament. He is a wonderfully complex mixture of opposites, mature to an inspiring degree, childish beyond recall, as in this instance; a man with a light, infectious approach to any subject that appeals, a terse, noncommittal observer, perfunctory of speech when confronted by someone or something that either offends or does not interest him; a man of compassionate understanding and entrenched prejudice. For him, a generosity of spirit far beyond the normal can be matched by a hidebound intransigence worthy of the most stubborn reactionary. He can be the extremes of the pendulum, which is perhaps why he can portray with conviction a wide assortment of humanity in his novels, but as a Saturday night companion in a Montrose, Colorado, supper club he can be the pits!

By morning he was revived and eager once more, and we rolled back to Denver after five most enjoyable days. On that trip I secured the only photograph I was ever able to take of Michener at rest, stretched out under a tree by the Virgin River in Zion National Park, his ever-present baseball-type cap pulled over his eyes to shut out the warm May sun glinting through the overhanging branches. He must have rested there for a full five minutes.

Four weeks later, on June 18, Tessa and I drove to St. Louis to meet Jim on his return from a 10-day fact-finding visit to Ireland. He had been persuaded to go on this trip, somewhat against his inclination, by a group of churchmen and laymen in Pennsylvania, and he had conceded his time in one of those selfless gestures of which he is capable. Jim was as concerned by the deadlock of opposing religious attitudes in the two Irelands as any non-Irish, non-Roman Catholic, non-Presbyterian could be, and his instinctive feeling that he was probably not best fitted to enter the fray as a writer on such a complex subject was borne out by his experience in that unhappy land. He returned saddened and perplexed, but not prepared to register complaint or accusation one way or another.

Jim had come to St. Louis to confirm certain aspects of the writing he had already completed on the early days of the city that stood at the confluence of the Missouri and Mississippi Rivers. Nothing now remained of the 18th-century buildings along the waterfront, and only the old French cathedral standing well back from the river linked us directly with the years of Pasquinel, Lisa and Papa Bockweiss. We talked at length with John Francis McDermott, a distinguished authority on the early days of St. Louis, and Jim came away satisfied that his determination of the St. Louis lifestyle two hundred years earlier was sound. Pasquinel was indeed a *coureur de bois,* not a *voyageur;* the solid rise to fortune of silversmith Herman Bockweiss was typical of German immigrants at a time when the city still had fewer than one thousand inhabitants; and so on. Michener was also checking that his attitude and approach in writing about that early era were valid, that the "weight" of the chapter was consistent with historical accuracy.

We returned from St. Louis via Hannibal, Macon, and Saint Joseph, Missouri, up the North Platte River, past Chimney Rock, Nebraska, that slim pinnacle of hope raised like a beckoning finger to immigrant wagons toiling across the plains, and finally to Fort Laramie, before turning south to Denver. It was nearly all ground that Jim had covered several times before, but he had now completed his first draft of Levi and Elly's journey and, like his St. Louis visit, he wanted to cross the region once more to confirm the tones of his narrative.

Our long-distance field trips covered many thousands of miles in a comparatively short time. They were, in a sense, periods of respite from the very concentrated pattern of day-to-day work in and around Denver. After our initial fears about travelling with Michener were allayed, we looked forward eagerly to each succeeding journey. While we drove, we discussed just about everything of current topic. We were an informed travelling forum on Watergate, women's lib, abortion, equal rights, black power, education, the legal system, Watergate, minorities, the economy, Vietnam, Watergate . . . Watergate . . . Watergate. You name it, we discussed it, in conversations punctuated with jellybeans, cookies, picnics, and constant referral to map after map as we ticked off the mileposts.

Sometimes Michener talked of his early life, about which I had known nothing, and I sensed that it had been a period of some difficulty, for it was the one area of his conversation that never had overtones of humor. All else, his teaching career, life in the Navy, his knowledge of Nixon and his administration, any reminiscence was grist for humorous anecdote, but never his early childhood. Not until much later did I learn that he was abandoned as a newborn baby, brought up by a foster mother who was forced from time to time to take her charges to the poorhouse for shelter when all the money ran out; that he has never known the identity of his real mother and father. He never mentioned those facts, but touched only on the strong aspects of his childhood, the stern Quaker upbringing imposed by his wonderful mother, for he knew Mrs. Michener only as such, until the time when he was eighteen years old that she told him of his infancy. He talked of the sports coach who encouraged him to win a basketball scholarship to college, and he constantly referred to all the good things that society did for him, never that anything had been denied him.

I mentioned this because it is the key to understanding Michener. He is forever grateful for the chances he has been given in life, and he is driven to repay society

Mexican mesquite lands stretch southward from the border
towards Chihuahua, where we researched the legend of

Pancho Villa for whom such country provided refuge
between his marauding raids.

over and over again for those opportunities. Now a man of some financial means, he remains acutely conscious of poverty, very careful with his money. Every dollar is a dollar, not some minute percentage symbol of total assets to be used carelessly or aimlessly. He remembers his poverty, remembers the guidance and kindness shown him as a child, and he works incessantly to prevent a recurrence of the first and to show his gratitude for the second. Add to those the love of learning instilled in him by Mrs. Michener, and it is not difficult to understand the motivations that have led to *Centennial* and a score of other titles.

But these are almost sombre thoughts, and they were never part of the lively conversations we had on the long journeys. Then, the only thing that brought tears to our eyes were the words of one of Michener's favourite old-time ballads, sung by an angelic choir on yet another of his home-taped cassettes:

> *"Soft as the Voice of an Angel,*
> *Breathing a Lesson unheard,*
> *Hope with a gentle Persuasion,*
> *Whispers her comforting Word.*
> *Wait till the Darkness is over,*
> *Wait till the Tempest is done,*
> *Hope for the Sunshine Tomorrow,*
> *After the Shower is gone."*

*Whispering Hope*, the theme song of the Wendells, never failed to delight us. Our work was certainly intense, but we laughed a lot, too, and one other song I will not easily forget was a Victorian music-hall ballad Jim had learned by heart many years before on a visit to Britain. We had been discussing differing traits of national humor, and Jim illustrated his love for Cockney pathos with a soulful recitation of this delicate air:

> *"They're moving father's grave to*
> *build a sewer,*
> *They're digging it regardless of expense,*
> *They're shifting his remains to make way*
> *for ten-inch drains,*
> *Just to titillate some rich toff's fundaments.*
>
> *"In life me father never was a quitter,*
> *I doubt that he will be a quitter now.*
> *He'll wrap up in a sheet and haunt that*
> *toilet seat,*
> *And they will defecate as he allows.*
>
> *"My word there's gonna be some constipation,*
> *And when it hits 'em they won't be so brave.*
> *They'll get what they deserve for havin' the*
> *bloody nerve,*
> *To muck about with a British workman's grave."*

This ditty, echoing incongruously across the Texas countryside, almost beat out *I Ride an Old Paint* as our favorite song — and that's saying something.

Professor Bertrand Schultz, of the University of Nebraska, Lincoln, Nebraska, ponders questions on early man.

Studying plowing patterns to retain topsoil moisture.

Talking cattle with Powder River rancher Bob Gibbs. (Photos © Tessa Dalton)

Michener patterned Temchic, the hometown of Tranquilino Marquez in *Centennial,* after this old silver-mining town of Cusihuiriachi, west of Chihuahua, Mexico. Now largely deserted, the town still boasted this lone horseman we encountered, and a gaggle of mischievous imps Jim befriended. The ruined town evoked feelings of a turbulent past, and I was content to leave it to its secrets. (Photos © Tessa Dalton) In the right-hand photograph, Michener's companions are Tessa Dalton and our local guide.

# CHAPTER III

## DENVER AND THE SHORT FORAYS

hree sites in the west came close to shattering my respect for James A. Michener as a detached, objective researcher. Each of them made him irrational in his attitude toward them, overindulgent in his praise of them, and constant in his desire to return to them. They seduced him like three mistresses, located conveniently apart — none closer than a hundred miles from the next — and each with particular attractions he found impossible to resist. Whenever he was near them he would find an excuse to go to them — and always afterwards he was like a man revived.

One was the long-abandoned township of Keota, northeast of Greeley, Colorado, a monument to the dashed hopes of trusting men and women who came west to tame the prairies; one was Fort Laramie, the linchpin of the early discovery and settlement of the Rocky Mountains; and the third was The Satire Lounge, a Mexican restaurant on East Colefax in Denver. During the months we were working along the front range, we homed on these three sites like pigeons returning to roost.

Driving back to Denver from a meeting with grizzled old farmers in Sterling, Colorado, or from a visit to the northern extremities of the Venneford ranch along the Wyoming border, Jim would suddenly look up from his map and say, "Let's take a left at the next intersection," and from that point we would twist and turn through a maze of county roads until, sure enough, we came to Keota.

"I returned to Keota a score of times," he wrote, " — in blizzards, in spring when the flowers were out, at dusk as I was coming home from Cheyenne, or whenever I visited the buttes." One day, when he had an official luncheon to attend in Greeley, he asked me to drive to Keota that morning — it was only a detour of about eighty miles. With a spring snowstorm swirling around us, turning the county road into quagmires, we were losing both time and traction, but Jim would not be deterred. "It's not far now," he repeated a dozen times as we broke through successive snowdrifts, until at last we crossed the railroad track that marked the western limit of the town. We stayed there a full three minutes while Jim looked again at the forlorn remnants of the town, then we turned and forced our way back to his lunch meeting.

For Jim, Keota epitomized the promise and disaster of the 1920's and 30's he brings to life in the Drylands chapter of *Centennial,* and in truth it was a town that never had a chance. Settled in 1888, incorporated in 1919 with a population of 129, serving a surrounding area of struggling homesteaders doomed to failure, the skids were under it from the start. By 1930 its inhabitants had dwindled to 108 men, women and children, and by 1940 the dust storms had blown away all of its hope and all but 34 of its citizens. Its population was reduced from 34 in 1940 to 21 in 1950, to 13 ten years later, and to a total of six in 1970 — Clyde Stanley, the postmaster, and his sister Faye being two of those final caretakers.

It was the friendship and extraordinarily sharp memory of Clyde Stanley that brought Jim back time and time again, to the one communal spark of life left in the town — the post office. Stanley was a frail little man left over from a long-departed era; a gentle, scholarly, unkempt, shuffling figure burdened by the misdemeanours of fate, and he and his apple-cheeked sister Faye, a retired schoolteacher of intense vitality and irreverent wit, now ran a post office that looked more like a used bookstore than a government agency.

Two of its walls were lined from floor to ceiling with a selection of books on the west; in one corner stood the old printing press that had kept the town alive; along the third wall a phalanx of abandoned post-office boxes bore witness to the good news that never came to this town; and against a long window facing the street a few straggly geraniums searched the dusty windowpanes for light and sun. Yet for all its sense of decay, the Keota post office was a place of lively chatter and vivid reminiscence whenever we visited it. There Jim, his baseball cap tilted to the back of his head, and Clyde, his baggy pants supported by string, his bright eyes peering through dime-store spectacles, would sit by the hour discussing things that once had been, when men bore hope into the town and exchanged it all too quickly for ruin and despair. Stanley had seen it all, and Michener fashioned his Land Commissioner in *Centennial*, Walter Bellamy, after him, with respect and great affection.

Fort Laramie, west of Torrington, Wyoming, at the confluence of the Laramie and North Platte rivers, is a finely restored national historic site. If Keota represented the lost hope of the western immigrant homesteader, Fort Laramie in the early and mid-1800's stood forth in the rolling plains like a safe landfall at the end of a hazardous voyage. To its protective enclave came early trappers, traders and the westward wagons, often to spend the winter there before continuing in the following spring to Oregon and California. The Fort was the northern outpost of the white settlers' domain. North of it, all the way to Montana, was Indian country until late in the century. Today, situated in an unspoiled area of gently rolling country, the Fort still stands alone, and in the early-morning light, before the parking lot is filled, there is an atmosphere of historic time stood still.

To Jim, the Fort and its knowledgeable staff became a valuable center for research. In the sutler's store he restocked Levi's wagon with a variety of dried and preserved staples; a little to the southeast of the Fort he stood on the land where the tribes gathered for their great convocation; and a few miles west of the Fort, at Guernsey, he studied the names of immigrants scratched in the sandstone of Register Cliff, and walked in the wagon ruts worn deep in the limestone rock. Unlike Keota, the area had no feeling of melancholy. On the contrary, Fort Laramie stood as an omen of bright hope for all, that is, except the Indians on whose tribal grounds it trespassed.

On our return to Denver from Keota or Fort Laramie, Michener would frequently suggest that we visit his third love. "The Satire Lounge, incredible as it may seem from its name or its Humphrey Bogart decor," he wrote, "was the best Mexican restaurant in the west. To eat there was a privilege, for the food was prepared impeccably; it was hot enough to command respect, but not so fiery as to destroy digestion." His love for the Satire was even sufficient for us to cut out on a dressy reception given by the Governor of Colorado and hurry across town to place our order before the kitchen closed. It was surely the only occasion on which formal dress had been seen in our favorite cantina.

The Satire was rivalled only by Jim's occasional affection for Mr. Wong's Chinese restaurant, and by his utter devotion on Sundays to Wyatt's cafeteria.

Today, the only memorials to the community of Keota are in crumbling brick and peeling board, deserted dirt streets, and the rusting single-track railroad down which the last locomotive escaped to better times, leaving a dying town in its wake. The schoolhouse, where Michener in far off days addressed the graduating class, stands sentinel against a gentle blue sky once blackened by the duststorms that choked off both the livelihoods and hearts of homesteaders who vainly tried to tame the land. The town of Line Camp in *Centennial* drew much of its character from

Keota. *And worst of all, where were the homes that had been so painstakingly built, so painfully sustained during the years of drought? They were gone, vanished down to the building blocks of the cellars. A town which had had a newspaper and a dozen flourishing stores had completely* *disappeared. Only the mournful ruins of hope remained, and over those ruins flew the hawks of autumn.*—Chapter 14, *November Elegy*

## REGISTER CLIFF

The wayfarer's penchant for inscribing names and dates on prominent landmarks excites the interest of his descendants. Regretably, marks of historic value are often effaced by later opportunists.

Along the Oregon Trail, famed transcontinental route of the 19th century, pertinent dates are from the 1820's through the 1860's. Three outstanding recording areas exist within Wyoming: Register Cliff here; Independence Rock 180 miles west; and Names Hill a further 175 miles along the Trail's wandering course. Register Cliff and Names Hill are self-evident titles; Independence Rock derives from a July 4th, 1825 observance which, according to some authorities, was staged by Mountain Men of Fur Trade fame.

Register Cliff invited emigrants because broad river bottoms offered pleasing campsites and excellent pasture. Hardship and illness were inevitable to Trail travel; of 55,000 emigrants during a peak year some 5,000 died enroute. Cliffside graves attest to the high mortality. This being their lot, travelers eagerly sought and singularly valued recuperative lay overs. Here, rest offered the opportunity to register.

But not all who registered were worn and grieving emigrants. Early inscriptions were by Mountain Men inured to wilderness life -- many descendants of two centuries of French Fur Trade. One reads: "1829 This July 14". Does it denote an observance? If the American Independence Day was celebrated in 1825 at Independence Rock could the French trappers have noted Bastille Day at Register Cliff in 1829?

At left, names of wagon train emigrants carved on the face of Register Cliff, Guernsey, Wyoming.

Below, section of Oregon Trail in Wyoming. Even as late as 25 years ago, the trail was still littered with abandoned equipment from the wagons of a hundred years earlier. Old stoves, pots and pans, broken wheels, and the bleached timbers of wrecked prairie schooners, punctuated the miles between the lonely grave markers of emigrants who never reached the end of the journey.

The sutler's store (left), Fort Laramie, Wyoming, in a later building than that found by the *Centennial* wagon train in 1843, though the staples offered would have been the same. *They also wanted to purchase what dried meat they could to supplement the bacon, and they needed flour badly* . . . Chapter 6, *The Wagon and the Elephant.*

Wagon-wheel ruts (right) on the Oregon Trail at Guernsey, Wyoming, still suggest the physical exertion for man and beast that accompanied the westward trek.

In 1874-75, Army engineers built this iron bridge (below right) across the Laramie River, Wyoming, at a spot two miles north of Fort Laramie, close by the confluence of the Laramie and North Platte Rivers. A vital link in the development of the area, the timbers of its 420-foot span echoed to the clatter of the Cheyenne-Deadwood Stage, and allowed swift passage of military expeditions in the final Indian campaigns. In regular use until 1958, it is probably the oldest surviving military bridge west of the Mississippi, and is now preserved as a historic monument.

All photos © Tessa Dalton

Clyde Stanley, the old postmaster at Keota, Colorado, recalls for Michener the broken dreams of the Depression years. Stanley became Michener's prototype for Walter Bellamy in *Centennial's* chapter on dryland farming. In the final section of the book Walter Bellamy, too, was old: *Our car pulled up before one of the low stone buildings and Garrett got out to knock on the door. For a moment it seemed that no one was there. Then a very old man with fading reddish hair and deep-set eyes came to the door . . . He led us into the office from which he had once helped to give away a hundred and ninety thousand acres of dryland, and he had watched as the defeated had abandoned the land. Now only he survived. With firm voice he spoke of those distant years . . .* —Chapter 14, *November Elegy*

Before it closed its doors for the last time, Keota Post Office became a recurring landfall for Michener in his search for the old days. Time after time he would push open the door to seek from Clyde Stanley, and his sister Faye, the details that would help him recreate the story of the vanished town. (Photo © Tessa Dalton)

"Every Sunday I went there for my noonday meal. My fare was invariable: carrot-and-pineapple salad, Waldorf salad, dish of lima beans, two slices of fried eggplant, a glass of buttermilk, a wedge of cherry crumb pie. If I had to work in Denver for another hundred Sundays, I would stick to that same meal."

When we were not covering research in distant states and in Mexico, we were either holed up in Denver, blanketed with snow, or on a series of short one- or two-day trips in the vicinity. The narrowing down to find detail on any one subject took us to many different experts. Sometimes Michener split these responsibilities between us, but most often we would all concentrate on a particular aspect and cover it together. Visits to the Wyoming State Museum and Library in Cheyenne, to the western history research center at the University of Wyoming in Laramie, to the Wyoming Hereford Ranch, to experts on Shoshone and Arapaho tribal history, and to Fort Laramie helped answer our questions on the many sections of *Centennial* that overlapped from Colorado to Wyoming. What were the rules of the Cheyenne Club, how many acres were needed per cow and calf unit for efficient operation of the Venneford ranch, what troupes came to Cheyenne to perform in the thriving opera houses of the day, what were the timetables of early Union Pacific trains, did Moreton Frewen go bankrupt after the disastrous blizzard of 1887, how many sheep could fit into a boxcar in 1886?

During those winter months in Denver, Michener established a routine that allowed him not only to continue his research in the Denver libraries, visit numerous sites within a two-hundred-mile radius, talk with scores of experts, but also to write the final first draft of his novel. This organization of a dozen different activities called for the strict disciplines on which he thrives. In the mornings, from around 6:30 until just before noon, he would stab away at his manual typewriter, completing as much as 2,000 words in each session. At a regular lunchtime meeting in his apartment he would then brief Tessa Dalton and myself on his requirements for the twenty-four hours before our next meeting. This routine held good through all seven days of the week, and was broken only when we were absent on field trips.

Very important to Michener was a regular exercise session each afternoon at 5:30 in the gymnasium of the apartment building in which he was living. A regimen of 50 sit-ups and two miles on the bicycle was as important to him as his sessions at the typewriter, for he has always felt that anyone engaged in creative work should regard a good physical condition as vital to the production of one's best work. I was in fact surprised that he did not have a basketball hoop and a rowing machine set up in his study, for then the time-consuming journey to the basement and back would have been eliminated.

Throughout the months of work Mari Michener acted as a sort of super den mother, keeping track of Jim's copious mail, looking after all of us with a skillful blend of encouragement, advice, or remonstration when she felt that we were pushing ourselves beyond a sane limit of excess in our endeavors. As well as her journeys east to attend to domestic detail back home in Bucks County, Pennsylvania, she would often accompany us on field trips, and always she contributed much to the smooth progress of our working life.

The Denver Public Library came to know Mari almost as one of the staff, for each day when Jim was working in Denver she would go in search of reference books for him. He would say, "Mari, get me the three best books on sugar beet culture," or, "I need more material on Arapaho family life in the early 1800's," and soon she would return with a shopping bag bulging with new grist for the insatiable Michener mill.

In addition to all his writing and research activity, Jim served regularly on two commissions, one in Colorado, the second in Washington, travelled to Ireland, Alaska and New York, wrote a major article on Watergate for the *New York Times,* and took time off to watch on TV the Senate hearings on the Watergate scandal. The portent of Watergate and the attitudes and behaviour of top-ranking officials of the administration absolutely stunned Michener and drove him to what he has described as "the most difficult piece of writing I have ever engaged in, and perhaps the most important."

*I was interrupting my novel at a precarious time to do this essay only because I respected the* Times, *wrong though they could be at times, and I wanted to contribute even a mite to the crucial task of keeping our press free. I was quite convinced that Nixon's team had decided to humiliate the leading newspapers and utterly gut the television system. Anything I could do to combat this would be of significance, even though minor in weight, and I worked like a demon for two weeks, endeavoring to clarify my thinking and to state my position accurately.*

*At the end of a most trying period, during which I reviewed every sentence in the essay numerous times, refining my position, I produced a banged-up manuscript which I hand-carried east to deliver to Nadia for typing. It was the most accurate piece of writing I had ever done. . . . I have never worked so hard on anything before. It was an essay I wanted to write, that I had to write. I am glad that I stopped everything to work on this.*

Even those brief extracts from his notes on the article show the huge weight of his concern over Watergate. They also illustrate the basic principle upon which he works these days:

*I am not interested in writing anything which does not concern me immediately and deeply, and if I do write I want to do so in a way that summarizes all the knowledge I have at that moment. I believe that this is why I have stayed young in my attitudes, and to a lesser extent, why some of my pieces have been fairly substantial. I write in order to educate myself, to organize my thoughts, to discover the depth of my own convictions, to find out how far I am willing to commit myself in public.*

Watergate certainly claimed Michener's attention, yet anxiety about his country was one of the major reasons that led him to write *Centennial,* so that although he spent valuable time in the preparation of the Watergate article, he lost none of the head of steam he had worked up for his novel.

Before I joined him in Denver, he had completed first drafts of some of the early chapters of *Centennial,* and as early as January 17 he wrote to Albert Erskine at Random House: "I am now in Texas doing field work on several of the remaining chapters. They are all outlined in my head and practically written, save for the 585 pages and the quarter million words. In other words, the hard part's done! Seven typewriter ribbons later, it may all be done."

Within two months, on March 15, Erskine had written to Jim: "I finished a first quick-step (fast for me, probably slow for most people) reading of I through VIII just a little while ago. . . ." Between October 1972 and March 1973 Jim completed two thirds of *Centennial.* I cite this because it is difficult for people to understand a capacity for such intense work. Often I am told "on the best authority" that Michener uses about twenty researchers and writers in the preparation of a major novel. I can appreciate why anyone might arrive at this conclusion, yet it is quite simply not so. Prior to *Centennial* he had never had any full-time assistance in the

Of this photograph Michener wrote: "This lovely shot at Pawnee Buttes tells the whole story of the book." Of the buttes he wrote in *Centennial*: *They were extraordinary, these two sentinels of the plains. Visible for miles in each direction, they guarded a bleak and silent empire. They were the only remaining relics of that vast plain which the New Rockies had deposited; each bit of land the sentinels surveyed dated back to the ancient times before the mountains were born.*—Chapter 2, *The Land*

And of Herefords, he wrote: *His horns sloped down at a sharp angle, ending well below his eyes. His forehead was ample, studded with bone and covered with white curly hair. His snout was a healthy pale pink, and his mouth drooped as if he had a surly disposition, while down the back of his neck ran a heavy line of twisted white hair . . . Thanks largely to the pioneering efforts of the Venneford people, and Jim Lloyd's scrupulous attention to honest breeding, the Hereford became the noble animal of the west, and there were many like Jim whose hearts beat faster when they saw the range area populated by 'white-faces!'*—Chapter 10, *A Smell of Sheep*

preparation of a novel, and even in this instance he duplicated all the research we undertook. That he had us on hand certainly speeded up the completion of the manuscript, at his estimate probably by as much as a year, but without us it would to all intents and purposes have been the same novel. Michener will willingly adopt editorial suggestions on a finished manuscript, and indeed counts on them from his Random House team led by Albert Erskine, but the research and the writing are his own.

By March 27, Michener was so far ahead in his preparation that he was able to write to Erskine: "Because I have so much travel facing me I thought I ought to outline the last two chapters of the novel. Then, if anything hits me, the book could be finished." Michener went on to outline the Drylands chapter and November Elegy, the only two sections of the book he had not already completed in his first final draft:

## XIII.   Drylands

*Map shows the land from Centennial east, focusing on Grebe farm, lonely Homestead School.*

*In 1910 Colorado has a fine, balanced system of land usage: range, irrigation. Into this settled understanding explodes Dr. Creevey with his vision of dryland farming. Deep ploughing, impacting, harrowing, leveling: everything wrong. Sincere, honest, convinced he sweeps the rest. In Iowa convinces George Grebe.*

*Land is handled by Liberty Land. Weller's new brochure. Vast promises for a new town called Line Camp, situated near Line Camp Three and Rattlesnake Buttes. The awful beginnings. Creevey's whirlwind visits to inspire.*

*Homestead School and teacherage. Not a single visible thing in any direction. Mr. Bellamy.*

*Philip Weller concentrates on real estate and becomes wealthy. Cautious, prudent. Controls area.*

*Potato Brumbaugh, in 1911, is 82. He and Jim Lloyd, 57, fight the dryland idea, know it is wrong, predict disaster. Potato's death, stroke, aware that he never thought radically enough on either water or land. Jim Lloyd dies next day, Herefords.*

*Tranquilino Marquez' continuing role as beet worker, Denver for winter. Tough little Triunfador. Brumbaugh wants to educate him, parents say no. The cantina.*

*Max Brumbaugh gives up farm, turns to feeding cattle, using pulp from Central Sugar. Large feed yards. He and Weller have correct vision of future.*

*But now story focuses almost entirely on Grebes. The drylands. Rise and fall of Line Camp. Hopelessness as Creevey's ideas peter out.*

*Coming of the great dust bowl. Drylands in 1933–35. Events of 1936. Son Tim at stock show wrestling steer. Fails. Is awarded one by a rancher. Grooming for*

Nature is slowly eroding the remaining evidence of Keota, Colorado, and the efforts of men and women who tried to build a town that would one day become a city, and instead became a ruin within a lifetime. (Photo © Tessa Dalton)

*next year. How a family lives with no money. Dust. Mr. Bellamy. Spring on the prairie, dust, wind, Mrs. Grebe cuts throats her three youngest while Tim is at 1935 show. Her husband shoots her, puts shotgun in his own mouth. Tim finds.*

*Philip Weller buys Grebe place and other abandoned farms. Tries dryland wheat. Agony of rain or no rain 1935–36, 37, 38, 39. Vastly overextended but hopes for one good rain in 1939. Swears off, but early Sunday morning, September 1, 1939, hears on radio that Germany has invaded Poland. Buys all available land and tells his wife America will have to come in, and we'll need wheat. If the war lasts long enough, we'll make millions. If we get just rain.*

### XIV.   November Elegy

*A sketchy, day-by-day account of the month of November, 1974, focusing solely on Paul Garrett, 46 years old, and head of Vennefords. Instead of map, a genealogy, as if he were registered Hereford, as shown in notebook going back four generations. Dates follow.*

1. *Lame duck governor announces his appointment chairman commission for centennial.*

4. *Has to decide whether or not to vote for Clayton Weller for governor. Can't do it.*

6. *His reflections as he travels state. (This material already written, but in previous form as potential magazine excerpts. That idea not too good in working out all the ideas existing there to be used here.)*

14. *Events leading to his proposal to Flor Marquez, her father's cantina, the songs.*

16. *The marriage.*

17. *The Appaloosa Club, Nez Perce bit.*

21. *His apprehension about attending the Thursday luncheon of the Cattlemen's Club. His acceptance always been dubious because of sheep. Now Mexican wife. Warmly greeted. Announces in great confusion that on Friday he's seeing the Simmenthal man.*

22. *Simmenthal man. Cross-breeding of Herefords. His grief at passing of old order.*

23. *Long drive to Lincoln for Colorado-Nebraska game. Introduces wife. Sensational Colorado victory 20–14. Long ride home. Autos. Nebraska filling station man, and Big Red Nebraska sign. Entry into Colorado at Julesburg. Mountains clearer, air sweeter, Governor Weller will have easier time with legislature, prairie looks magnificent because Colorado won the football game.*

25. *Annual trip to Arapaho Reservation, Wyoming. He 3% Indian himself. Two husbands who died night before, drunk, froze to death ten feet from house. Old woman his relative. All but she drinking heavily.*

27. *Stop at Fort Laramie, as always. Splendid reconstruction. Recollections of his ancestors Pasquinel, Lame Beaver, Lucinda McKeag. Levi Zendt, Major Mercy, young Pasquinel Mercy hunting buffalo.*

28. *Back roads to Rattlesnake Buttes. Jim Lloyd and John Skimmerhorn as men who loved the land. Mr. Bellamy living in the magnificent, plain old church. Only one left at Line Camp.*

30. *Novel ends with section on Cisco Carpenter's reflections on Centennial as great place to live, pretty much as written.*

*This chapter to consist of Lewis Vernor's report on Garrett as typical of the area. Numerous blocked-in quotes, no quote marks, of things Garrett said when they were traveling together, into tape recorder. Footnoted first appearance something like this:*

*⁺ All inserted quotations in this chapter are from tape recording of Paul Garrett's voice as we traveled together during the month of November, 1974.*

*The whole to give an impression of the west as of now, with emphasis on the land and its prospects.*

*Jim Michener*

To decrease the possibility that these instructions might have to be followed, I tried to arrange our journeys so that Jim did as little of the driving as possible. The lethal potential of Michener behind the wheel is not to be underestimated.

By any measurement, what he achieved during that winter was a prodigious amount of work, and of course some things along the way went by the board. He could be curt, distant, and so totally preoccupied with matters in hand as to be unreasonable in his demands. Weekends and holidays were all treated equally as workdays, which we quite readily accepted, but he could throw an overnight work load at you that was almost indigestible. Only the knowledge that he was not even aware of the extent of his demands prevented resentment. Most of the time he cared little about what he ate, he never drank coffee, rarely touched alcohol. When he was left to his own devices he would dress in whatever first came to hand — often, around the apartment, in baggy shorts and an unharmonious shirt. Michener will never make the list of the world's best-dressed men and, at his not infrequent worst, he looks like an advertisement for a thrift shop.

Everything became subordinate to the work in hand, though the work itself was frequently enjoyable. In Colorado we went on some good field trips. On an early-morning bird walk east of Fort Collins, with Dr. Gus Swanson of Colorado State University, we found Michener's favorite, the avocet, and the rare burrowing owl. On another trip we climbed to the headwaters of the Grand Ditch, far up Poudre Canyon; on yet another we met with Bertrand Schultz of the University of Nebraska at the famous Agate Springs fossil site in western Nebraska, and picked through the bones of rhinoceros and camel that had once roamed the western plains. Wherever we went it was important to Michener to have as close as possible contact with the things he would describe in his book. He would taste the water, chew a little on the gamma grass the buffalo liked best, grub on his hands and knees in the beet fields and the wheat fields to understand the labors of Brumbaugh's Mexicans or the

The rich variety of Plains' grass supported, from time immemorial, a plethora of wildlife. Here, at Homestead National Monument, Beatrice, Nebraska, Michener studies blue grama, favorite grazing of the long departed buffalo. (Photo © Tessa Dalton)

Ash Hollow, Nebraska, a famous landfall for emigrant wagon trains. Thousands of these wagons pressed onward from Ash Hollow to Fort Laramie, leaving ruts so deeply embedded on the 'highway' that they remain today (center photo), indelible reminders of the surge to reach America's far western lands. (Photos © Tessa Dalton)

Chimney Rock, Nebraska. In the century and a quarter since the wagon treks it has been scaled down by wind and rain, but it is still visible from many miles distance, an unmistakable marker on the route west. *They came Chimney Rock, a needle pointing skyward; and Scott's Bluff, shame of the west, where early trappers had been accused of abandoning a sick partner named Scott, leaving him to die alone; and then the vast and open land where Indians were on the move.*—Chapter 6, *The Wagon and the Elephant*

Old time farmers at Sterling, Colorado, remembered the old days. Otto Unfug, to whom Michener dedicated *Centennial,* is on the left of the photograph, next to Mari Michener. Behind them is Tessa Dalton.

Jim and Mari Michener in Douglas, Wyoming, *home of the fabled jackalope, half-jackrabbit, half-antelope. Local taxidermists were so skilled at grafting small deer horns onto the heads of stuffed jackrabbits that many visitors, including Flor Garrett, believed the mutant existed. A huge statue in the town square confirmed her belief* . . . Chapter 14, *November*

*Elegy.* Some say that the shy jackalope, seen rarely even by the sharp eyes of early-day cowboys, is now extinct. Others, in any bar throughout the state, will swear that it shows itself to those who truly believe in it—but, even then, only in the most demanding conditions of light and distance. (Photo © Tessa Dalton)

In the realm of the mountain men, Jim Michener, and Tony Bevinetto of the National Park Service, look across Jackson Lake toward the Tetons. (Photo © Tessa Dalton)

plight of the sod farmer whose fields were blown away in the great dust storms of the Depression.

The Federal Center in Denver was a constant source of information for Michener on geology, paleontology, national parks and water resources. In notes on the preparation of *Centennial* that he wrote for free and limited distribution by Random House among librarians and booksellers only, he states:

*Four men at the Center exerted a deep influence on my thinking, and when I describe their fields of scholarship, you will see the directions in which my mind was working. Merril J. Mattes was a tall, quiet man who worked for the National Park Service, and during many decades spent at various western forts he had acquired a phenomenal body of information on the trails that crossed Nebraska and Wyoming, particularly the one leading to Oregon. On a field trip he was remarkably perceptive; talking in a library he could evoke whole periods of history. He was the kind of scholar our government employs at many different levels, lending distinction to whatever they touch.*

*John E. Moors was a much different kind of man, younger, more volatile, scintillating in conversation. His specialty was water; he probably knew as much about the reserves of the west as any man in America, and to work with him was an exploration of clashing ideas and projections far into the future.*

*Ogden Tweto was a small, tightly compacted man who had specialized in one thing: how the new Rocky Mountains evolved some forty million years ago. He himself was like granite, very cautious in delivering an opinion, most judicious in evaluating the theories of others. He was a meticulous editor and would allow no generalization to pass unchallenged. In his field he was unparalleled.*

*The man I remember most, however, was a tall, acidulous gentleman of the old school who wore a vest and spoke with such quiet force that he annihilated his opposition. G. Edward Lewis was a Yale man, and while by no means old he was scarred from academic battle. Ideas to him were precious; facts were not to be violated. He was courtly, gifted with a tremendous vocabulary, and infuriating in debate. I remember taking a portion of my novel to him, the part dealing with dinosaurs, and I was especially proud of a long section in which I depicted this grand diplodocus, eighty feet long, emerging from the swamp and walking at last in full view to browse some trees.*

*"Splendid piece of writing," Lewis said. When I nodded modestly, he added, "But I suppose you know that such dinosaurs never walked on land?"*

*I was aghast. I had worked long on this section and had consulted at least seventeen paintings showing my specific dinosaur stalking majestically across imaginary cretaceous landscapes. "Merely the guesswork of the painter," Lewis snorted. "Wanted to display the entire skeleton of the beast."*

*When I argued that all the painters couldn't have been wrong, he said, "When you rely solely upon your imagination you're usually wrong." And he took me into his study, where he had spread out some three dozen learned journals, and very patiently he went over each one with me, until I was convinced that the joint-pads of diplodocus were so fragile that they would probably not have sustained the creature had it wanted to walk on land. Somewhere in my papers I have a perfectly stunning description of my dinosaur emerging from the swamp, but Lewis would not let me publish it, and whenever I argued with him about buffalo or rattlesnakes or the forerunners of the bison, out would come the research studies, and I would be forced to revise my thinking.*

*This peak should have been called Beaver Mountain, but unfortunately, men are sometimes not imaginative . . . the best mountain of them all, with a little beaver crawling up its flank, was given the drabbest name of all—Long's Peak.*—Chapter 3, *The Inhabitants*—Michener has been challenged, even by Coloradoans, on the existence of the stone beaver, but it is certainly there for all to see. I took this shot from Estes Park in mid-May when the melting snow emphasized the solid substance of the little animal. The reproduction is exactly as it was photographed, and has not been retouched in any way.

We searched for two hours before Michener found a setting that suited him for the Kansas outlaw attack. *A band of sixteen Kansas outlaws led by the two Pettis boys swept in from a nest of low hills . . .*—Chapter 8, *The Cowboys*—

The western states are still littered with bleached and abandoned homesteads and townships whose best-laid plans went wrong. The restored cabin at Homestead National Monument, Beatrice, Nebraska, shows clearly the paucity of material possession that accompanied even 'successful' settlement of the plains; while the main street scene at Piedmont, Wyoming, a small community along the Union Pacific Railroad, shows the nostalgic flotsam that failure leaves behind. (Photos © Tessa Dalton)

During the time we spent in Denver, Michener kept up a continuous flow of correspondence: to his New York editor, to various experts from whom he needed advice, in replies to unending requests he received to write articles or to talk on aspects of his life and work, and for his own pure pleasure in passing comment on a wide range of subjects that interest him.

Michener has an extraordinarily retentive memory, which he makes use of not only for his novels but in his vivid reminiscences of times spent in many parts of the world. He can tell a story as well verbally as he does on paper, and can recall names and facts and events with extraordinary clarity. Often when we were travelling he would regale us with these memories of people and places that had particularly appealed to him.

Perhaps most of all, he holds affection for rogues. Their skillfully conniving minds fascinate him; he holds a sort of reverse admiration for a man who can live by his wits alone. Oliver Wendell, in *Centennial,* fits the category, and unlike the bad men of the "westerns" who always pay for their misdeeds, Wendell goes from strength to strength — ending his life as a rich and respected citizen.

Perhaps in Jim's experience the smooth operator more often than not gets away with it, but whatever, he loves to watch them at work. In one instance he went to the trouble of recording his delight at his own Turkish publisher. To the front of a paperback edition of one of his books he pasted the following comment, covering a torrid illustration the like of which had never before been seen on a Michener book:

JAMES MICHENER

I always think of Turkey with a special sense of wonder and downright amazement. When I was a young man I went to Istanbul and was met in my hotel by a most ingratiating man who informed me that he was my Turkish publishers, and he show ed me four or five of my titles to prove it.

I could not recall having signed any contracts with him, so I began to ask some circuitous questions, but he forestalled me wucikly by saying, 'Oh, we don't bother with contracts. We're not members of the Feneva Convention so we just publish whatever we like. Somerset Maugham w was furious about it.'

He had come to my hotel to find out 'what I would like him to plagiarize next.' Delightful man.

But his present gambit outdoes all that went before. He's publishing my <u>Drifters</u> as a tract on lesbianism, and how by God he figured that out I simply cannot guess. There is, so far as I know , not a single statement or impression in the book that would substantiate this approach, but he says that Turks expect American novels to be pretty filthy, so the covers have to reflect that condition. None of the latest novels he's plagiarized dealt with lesbianism, so he thought mine mine might be a good candidate.

There ought to be a place in the world for Turkey. There ought to be a place in international publishing for my admiring friend. Trouble is, I admire him so much more than he does me.

J. A. M.

Jim always seemed to be able to take time for these light touches. At the height of the Watergate hearings he pinned up the front cover of a weekly news magazine — *Time* or *Newsweek* — which showed profiles of Haldeman and Erlichman wearing dark glasses and peering intently into the distance. From the bristle-topped head of Haldeman, Jim had drawn a speech balloon with the phrase, "Have the Allies Landed?" — his apt comment on the fascism that so nearly prevailed in Washington.

More often, however, his letters related to *Centennial*. The following is a typical example. It was written on May 6, 1973, at a time when he had all but completed his first draft of the novel, and it refers again to the problem of the Clovis and Folsom points and to research that he thought he had long since resolved. It shows the extent to which Michener keeps his options open at all stages of his preparation of a novel. It is a round-robin letter written collectively to six scientists with whom he had been working:

*Dear Drs. Wormington, Schultz, Stout, Lewis and Messrs. Crabtree, Bradley:*

*I write to you seeking brief counsel, which can be forwarded on a postcard, if necessary. I am in love with a mastodon and a Folsom point, and I don't know how to resolve the crisis!*

*I had pretty well finished my material on the introduction of early man to the area when Marie Wormington discovered that I was not dealing with the mastodon, and she felt that this was a most grievous lapse. She convinced me that I should at least re-study the whole problem.*

*But if I use the mastodon, I cannot use the Folsom point and will have to move two or three thousand years backward to the Clovis point.*

*As Crabtree and Bradley know, having seen that I wrote about the artistic merits of the Folsom point, I am much addicted to its beauty. But when I discussed the matter briefly with Drs. Schultz and Stout on a recent visit to Lincoln, they showed me that the Clovis could also be a beautiful object and I have since thought that my concepts could almost as easily be applied to it.*

*My question on which I seek your counsel is twofold: A. Is the Clovis-mastodon relationship preferable since it is older and involves a Pleistocene mammal which has vanished? B. If the Clovis is preferable, which specific type of Clovis should I use and and where can I find the very best representation of the type recommended? (I have access to most of the standard books on the subject.)*

*To Mr. Crabtree I would say that I have not yet rewritten the point section in light of his comments, but I would suppose that they apply equally well to the Clovis, should I decide to adopt it. I certainly thank him for his attention to detail. Working in the relative dark, as I often must for a spell, makes me doubly appreciative of expert counsel.*

*To Mr. Bradley, you almost torpedoed this whole letter! Just as I was writing it I received from the postman your letter with the Folsom point, and it looks even better than I remembered. I would appreciate your counsel on this matter.*

*To all. I notice as I finish this letter that the INQUA journal uses as its rubric a beautifully drawn Folsom point, so I apparently am not alone in appreciating the quality of this particular work. However, I have recently seen some Clovis points that were most handsome, so I am prepared to make the shift.*

*Just finished attending the two-day conference of geologists concentrating on the Laramide orogeny and was delighted with how many papers related specifically to things I was concerned with.*

*Most warmly,*
*Jim Michener*

In Yellowstone National Park Michener studied the buffalo, mainstay of Indian life through countless generations until the white man all but wiped them out. In *Centennial*, Broken Thumb laments: '*Once they were more plentiful than our ponies . . . Where have the buffalo hidden? Like us, they cannot stand the white man's ways and have left their old grounds . . . And when the buffalo are gone, we shall starve, and when we are starving, you will take away our lands, the tipis will be in flames and the rifles will fire and we will be no more. The great lands we have wandered over we will see no more.*'—Chapter 7, *The Massacre*

The great red tide of Nebraska football supporters at the game against the University of Colorado, in Lincoln, Nebraska, 1973. We drove there from Denver to experience at first hand this annual clash of adolescent juggernauts that Michener recounts in Chapter 14, *November Elegy: Here you have the citizens of two great states growing apoplectic about a football game played not by their own people, but by hired thugs imported at great expense from all over the United States . . . And for one Saturday afternoon in November the prestige of two states depends upon their performance. And the whole damned thing is done in the name of education.* (Photo © Tessa Dalton)

Many such letters, sent out to various experts, show the extent to which Michener is in love with the acquisition of knowledge far beyond its requirement as information for inclusion in his writing.

In addition to his letters seeking advice, Jim kept up a detailed and comprehensive correspondence with Albert Erskine on the progress of the book. These letters give great insight into the way Michener works, and a fraction of them is included at the end of this book, in the appendix.

Toward the end of July 1973, the first draft of *Centennial* written, Michener returned to Pennsylvania. In the fall of 1973 he was with us again, on a long field trip to Dinosaur National Monument in Utah, to sloth caves perched above the Colorado River on the northern fringes of the Grand Canyon, and to Los Angeles, where we studied the La Brea tarpit discoveries of mammoth, sabre-toothed tiger and other mammals that vanished from North America in the last Pleistocene extinction some 14,000 years ago.

Part of this work was a follow-up revision for *Centennial,* part of it for a long article he was preparing on the Pleistocene disappearance. And part of it, I knew, was an excuse to come west again. At the end of that trip we dug for mammoth fossils with George Frison in the great basin of Wyoming between the Big Horn mountains and the Wind River range, and we experienced the melee of the Nebraska-Colorado football game — our final item of research.

During the course of our travels, Levi Zendt had pushed almost 2,000 miles in search of a better life, Pasquinel had paddled the length of the South Platte and back, several times over during his curiously lonely life. And we had come a long way, too.

A meeting with cattlemen at Cody, Wyoming, to discuss modern crossbreeding trends. One of these ranchers, Malcom Wallop on the extreme right of the photograph, is now a U.S. Senator for Wyoming. The author is on Michener's left. (Photo © Tessa Dalton)

# CHAPTER IV

# THE WRITING

chener describes his approach to a novel as a series of concentric, decreasing circles, each one a distinct stage in the total preparation. The outside circle represents his initial study and reading on the project, a process that occupies many months. This leads to the second circle, his thinking of the subject in terms of main themes. The third circle in his selection of specific aspects of those main themes — in the case of *Centennial,* say, the Goodnight-Loving cattle trail, irrigation, the Russian farmer, the Depression, and so on; plus first thoughts on main biographical treatments, such as the Pawnee, the Sioux, the Mexicans, etc. This third circle covers a period of much trial and error in building up the main characters and episodes to fill out his planned chapters. For *Centennial,* it was work he had completed before he moved to Colorado.

In his original thinking, Michener considered the railroad as a unifying force for his novel, but a great deal of research convinced him that the building of the railroad was essentially a repetitive and predictable event, lacking sufficient overall drama. So he dropped his chapter on the story of the Union Pacific and its Chinese labor — the latter would have been his focus on the human aspect of the story. The railroad still plays a very important part in the story of *Centennial,* for activity around the railroad station in each community was the focus of rural life. This part he developed, but the actual tracklaying, mile by mile, he abandoned. At one stage he also had given some thought to a chapter on the gold fields, but he consistently drew back from that idea, feeling that the period had been covered many times.

The fourth diminishing circle covered his journeys, to find out where his cattle would cross the Llano Estacado, where the Pettis gang would attack the trail herd, and all the physical detail that made up that chapter and all the others. In this period he was building up his visual images for the story line that he had already firmly decided upon. The last and fifth circle is when he commits his research and his storehouse of visual images to paper. At this point he writes predominantly without reference to research material, for by this time he knows his story and his facts like an actor ready for the stage. He does refer to pasted-up maps, however, almost hourly during the writing of a novel: "It is of extreme importance to me to have complete maps of what I am writing about, and I go to considerable pains to collect them so that I can see a total situation at a glance."

Having completed stages one through four, he had one more major consideration to decide upon before he sat down to his typewriter:

*The time was at hand when I had to decide what kind of book this was to be — not what the content should be, for I had long ago determined that, but what the structure must be. I must be able to visualize the end product as a total work in which every item has its proper and subordinate place, and in which each interrelates with the other. If I have not identified this appropriate structure, I waste my time if I try to write, for I will produce nothing.*

*The technical problem was simply stated: I proposed telling a story with a tremendous time span, with incidents widely separated, and with whole new sets of characters required for every new chapter. To bind this together, and to encourage the reader to stay with this massive development of concept and idea, I knew I needed a central organizing thread.*

*I found it by basing my story on a learned man from the state of Georgia who is sent to Colorado by a magazine to report on the scene as he sees it in 1973, against his own rich background in American history. The first chapter would establish this gentleman; chapters two through thirteen would consist of reports back to his employers in New York, and the final chapter would represent the impact of all this material on both him and the last major character in his report.*

*At the conclusion of each of my twelve long stories I would add a series of foot-notes which would extend the narrative, throw light into corners of it, and correct misimpressions that might have gathered. I wanted the reader to catch an oblique view of something which had already been seen in another light earlier on. These notes were not added as afterthoughts — although sometimes they were useful in protecting me from misinterpretation — but were constructed from the beginning as an inherent part of the storytelling technique. They are the threads of reflection which tie the pages together.*

*The purpose of a writer like me — and I am a peculiar one not well fitted to serve as a model for others — is to create a universe to which the reader must surrender himself totally for an extended period of time. If he will do so, he will acquire under-standings, images and memories which will rest with him for a long time. The crea-tion of this universe requires all the art the writer can command; it is a painstaking task which cannot be done quickly, and every component of the finished book must contribute to the illusion.*

*In 1972, when I started the actual writing of* Centennial, *I had already lived with the Platte River for thirty-six years, and I wanted all men and women who read my account of its wandering across the plains to become as familiar with it as I was. The mountains had been my associates for three decades, and they would be characters in any story I elected to tell; especially the prairie, reaching to the horizon in all quarters, had been an object of love, and I intended to write of it in that way. These were the components of a tremendous universe, one that I wanted every reader to share. I wanted the west that I would be writing about to be real, and to achieve this, the reader had to follow the trails I had followed and see the land as I had seen it.*

While he was living in Greeley in the 1930's three of the major themes of *Centennial* became indelibly impressed on his mind — the geology of the region, the sugar-beet industry, and the plight of the Mexican labor force in Colorado:

Jim Michener, in search of *Centennial* east of Greeley, Colorado. (Photo © Tessa Dalton)

View from Michener's apartment in Denver where he wrote
*Centennial*. Throughout a winter of record-breaking snow-

falls, these white-capped roofs echoed the snowpack on
the distant mountain peaks. (Photo © Tessa Dalton)

*From the moment I started thinking about a book on Colorado, I visualized the story in terms of compelling human beings, men, women and children. My problem would be to eliminate, not invent, for I had lived, and sometimes intimately, with my potential characters. My problem was aggravated, however, by my additional determination to use inanimate objects and animals as characters.*

*First of all, I wanted to deal with the birth and death of the great mountains of the west, for it was they who established the quality of life at Centennial. I wanted also to deal with the river, for I saw it an artery along which the life of the area pulsed. And I did not intend to treat these majestic characters either quickly or lightly, for they formed the permanent framework of my story.*

*Next, I would have no interest in writing a novel about Colorado unless the animals which shared the land with the men were given equal attention. Centennial may be the only novel in which the spiritual values are first exhibited through the life of a dinosaur; I have grown to treasure diplodocus, who dominates Chapter 3, as much as any human I have created in my fiction.*

Michener's love of narrative can be traced directly to his early years, when, in the evenings, his mother would read to her charges stories from Dickens, Thackeray and others of the classics. His preference, still today, is mainly for 19th-century novelists, as is evident in his choice of the twelve works he considers necessary reading for a good grounding in fiction.

| | |
|---|---|
| Charles Dickens: | *Great Expectations* |
| W. M. Thackeray: | *Vanity Fair* |
| Honoré de Balzac: | *Le Père Goriot* |
| Leo Tolstoy: | *Resurrection* |
| Gustave Flaubert: | *Madame Bovary* |
| Ivan Goncharov: | *Oblomov* |
| Samuel Butler: | *The Way of All Flesh* |
| Arnold Bennett: | *Old Wives' Tale* |
| Erich Auerbach: | *Mimesis* |
| Virginia Wolff: | *To the Lighthouse* |
| Albert Camus: | *The Plague* |
| Ross Lockridge: | *Raintree County* |

He readily agrees that his style as a novelist is far closer to the 19th century than to contemporary writing.

Michener wrote *Centennial* at a large plain oak desk, on which were a small map, a dictionary, a spelling dictionary, Crabbe's English synonyms, a Bible, and a small reading lamp taped to the top of a Texsun unsweetened orange-juice can to give it added height. Also on it were one or two of his cube puzzles for diversion. He types a very full page, wasting no space whatsoever. His double-spaced manuscript begins at the very top of the page, his lines fall off the right-hand edge, and he continues until the last possible line is crammed in at the foot. He completes about seven of these pages a day, and his habit is not to work at the typewriter for more than a five-hour span in the mornings. If he has not completed some minor parts of research on a chapter, but feels ready to type his first draft, he "fudges" it, writing "as if" — two of his favorite expressions. He will then correct the version when he reworks his first draft, usually in handwritten capitals in ink. The actual writing of a chapter comes relatively easily, for Michener knows exactly what his chapter is going to contain before he begins. The long process of learning everything possible on his subject culminates in a speedy, relatively painless period of writing, though this is then followed by months of careful revision and editing.

Our long journeys with Michener between January and July 1973 occupied 44 days out of a total of 212. Another 40 or so were spent in overnight stays in Colorado and southern Wyoming, or on day-long field trips within a hundred-mile radius of Denver. Michener himself was additionally absent from the scene for a total of around 20 days, in which he went to Washington to serve on a presidential committee, to Alaska to receive an honorary degree, to New York to review work on the book with his Random House editor, and to Ireland. This meant that in a hundred or so writing days he not only gave us almost daily time to discuss and research segments of the book, but he also wrote the first draft of seven chapters of *Centennial*. He had completed the first draft of five chapters between October 1972 and January 1973, when we joined him.

He did not necessarily write the chapters in sequence, though in principle this was his aim. In practice it depended on the progress of our research, so that at times there would be minor sections of a chapter to go back over and fill in, at others, whole segments to complete. This was purely a matter of logistics, for the whole pattern of the book was so clearly defined in Michener's mind, incident by incident, chapter by chapter, by the time he was ready to write it, that to all intents and purposes he could begin his narrative at any point.

By the end of October 1972 he had mailed to Nadia for clean typing the first 17 pages of Chapter II, The Land, this in essence being the first chapter proper in the story of *Centennial*, following his opening chapter, The Commission. During November he added a further 12 pages of Chapter II, 58 pages of Chapter III, 54 pages of Chapter IV, and 25 pages of an article for the *New York Times*, "The Red Kimono."

Jim kept an exact track of his work as it progressed, entering in a small notebook each segment mailed to Nadia — the number of pages sent, the chapter, the date. Nadia then replied with a series of cards acknowledging the date received, which Jim then added to his little notebook. In December, Jim mailed 20 pages of Chapter I, 45 pages of Chapter V and a further 59 pages of Chapter IV. This system of "bookkeeping" was subject to the normal frailties of the postal service and the participants at either end of the pipeline, so that on January 16 Nadia sent the following card:

> *Dear Jim,*
>     *No. 9 — Section VII — Rec'd 1/15 p. 1–57*
>     *Your envelope was marked No. 10 on this. When I discussed*
> *the matter with Hercule P., he deduced by referring to your*
> *letter that you had originally intended to send Section VI*
> *first and had the envelope preaddressed, but VII materialized*
> *sooner, so that envelope 10 was sent prior to envelope 9.*
>     *Anyway, I'm bringing this to your attention in case an envelope*
> *is missing (and laughing my head off as I'm typing this). I*
> *am looking forward to seeing the number on Section VI, since my*
> *9 is your 10. But if XIV is next, we're finished.*
>                                 *Definitely, D.D.S.\**
>     *P.S. When this is all over, it might be fun to compare notebooks.*

* Once when Nadia proved especially obstreperous, he referred to her as "my dipsy-doodle secretary," a designation she appropriated.

The Tetons, haunt of the early day mountain men, were the farthest western range of the Rocky Mountains that Michener wrote of in *Centennial. The Rockies . . . have the*

*extravagent beauty of youth, the allure of adolescence, and they are mountains to be loved.*—Chapter 2, The Land)

Typical pages from many notebooks filled by Michener during the writing of *Centennial*. (All photos © Tessa Dalton)

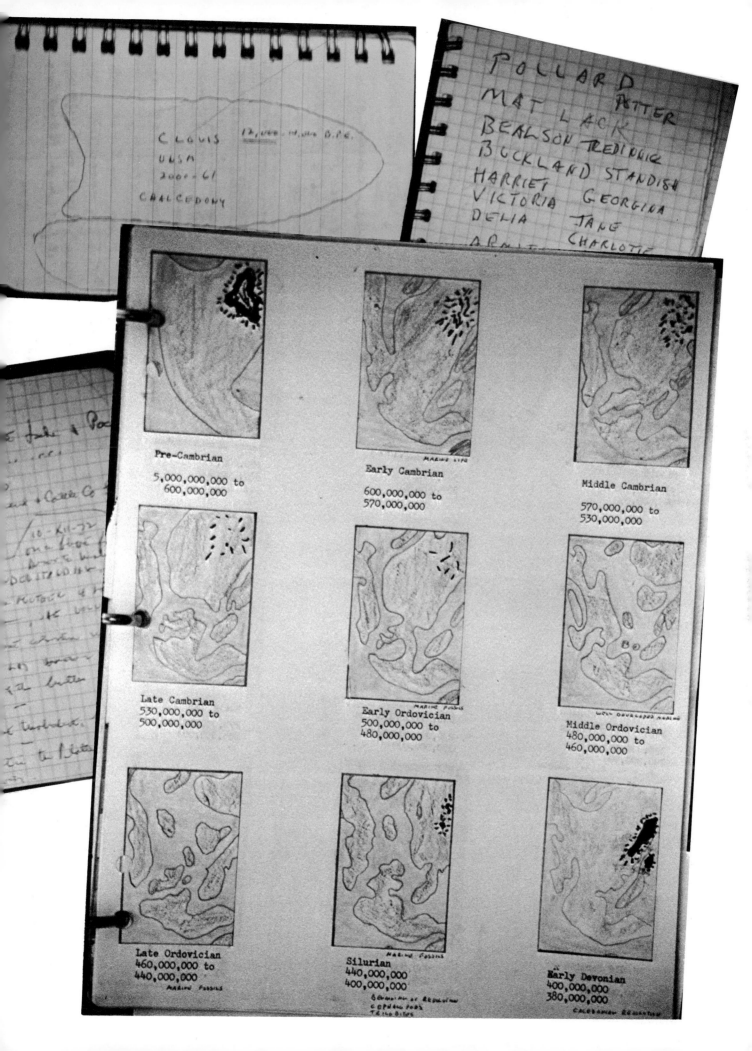

CLOVIS
UNSM
2001-61
CHALCEDONY

12,000 14,000 B.P.?

POLLARD PETTER
MAT LACK
BEALSON TREDINNIC
BUCKLAND STANDISH
HARRIET GEORGINA
VICTORIA JANE
DELIA CHARLOTTE
ARMIT

Pre-Cambrian

5,000,000,000 to
600,000,000

Early Cambrian

600,000,000 to
570,000,000

Middle Cambrian

570,000,000 to
530,000,000

Late Cambrian
530,000,000 to
500,000,000

Early Ordovician
500,000,000 to
480,000,000

Middle Ordovician
480,000,000 to
460,000,000

Late Ordovician
460,000,000 to
440,000,000

Silurian
440,000,000
400,000,000

Early Devonian
400,000,000
380,000,000

The Brazos River, southwest of Jacksboro, Texas, was the first barrier the longhorns had to cross on the long trail to Colorado. In *Centennial*, Michener calls the South Platte River, (below) . . . *a sad, bewildered nothing of a river* . . .

*It carries no great amount of water, and when it has some it is uncertain where it wants to take it.*—Chapter 2, *The Land*

—(Photos © Tessa Dalton)

The Red River, most aptly named of all the rivers we crossed in our research for the cattle trail, forms the long boundary between Oklahoma and Texas. The Purgatoire River, Colorado: . . . *practical men from Indiana and Tennessee, adapt-* *ing the sound to their own tongue, called it* Picketwire. *It was not a difficult river to cross* . . .—Chapter 8, *The Cow-boys*

(Photos © Tessa Dalton)

Ten days later Nadia further clarified the point by writing: "So my deduction was correct — your 10 is my 9, or is it the other way around?"

Things must have become clear to one or the other, for the postcards multiplied, the book grew. By March 7 the first drafts by Chapters I through VIII had been completed, typed clean and sent to Albert Erskine at Random House. Three months later all except portions of the last chapter were finished.

At the end of each completed chapter Nadia would send to Jim a detailed timetable of the events of that chapter for his easy cross-reference as he worked on others.

I am dwelling on this aspect of Jim's way of working because it shows the extent to which he thrives on complexity. His own notes outlining the various steps in the preparation of the manuscript show this love of detail quite clearly:

*My final first draft looks very sloppy, and it is. But it is also a working draft, on which I have scratched out and added to frequently, until is has grown like a healthy tree. This is where I have done my work, and I do not think I could change my working habits at this late date, merely in the interest of neatness.*

*My curious habit of pasting additions to pages stems from the fact that when I draft a chapter the very first time, I generate a tremendous kinesthetic sense, so that I know exactly where page 17 is, how it looks, what is on it, and how it relates to other pages. Were I, in retyping, to lose that eidetic numbering system, I would feel badly thrown off balance; so as far as possible I like to retain each original page numbering, altering and adding to it as required. Occasionally I am not able to retain the original system, but when I deviate it is almost always to my detriment.*

*My secretary keeps a magnifying glass to decipher my notes. I print them because I cannot myself read my hurried handwriting, and sometimes not even my carefully studied one.*

The illustrations on pages 140–141 show typical pages of original manuscript in the condition that they would be sent to Nadia Orapchuk for clean typing. Michener's notes continue:

*The clean typed copy is sent to Albert Erskine, and on it he does his first editorial work. As I work over the carbon copy I send Erskine corrected pages, which he inserts into his official copy. The carbon copy is the version on which I do a good deal of my revision. It was also read, in this instance, by numerous experts, by Kings and Dalton and Laird and by anyone whose opinion we consulted. Sometimes the entire chapter was sent out, sometimes only a few pages, and sometimes a xerox of the original. But on this version everyone away from the Random House office did a great deal of work. None was submitted to Erskine, however, without my having vetted it and usually recasting the corrections into my own words. When I finished with such work, I airmailed the whole chapter with all corrections to Erskine, to be incorporated into the final version of the manuscript.*

*After months of hard work by both him and me and also by Bert Krantz, the excellent and learned copy editor, this version will go to the typesetter to be set into galleys, but by that time it won't look very much like what it did at the start, for whole new sections will have appeared, old sections will have been chopped out, and innumerable corrections by all of us will have been inserted, weighed and sometimes thrown out again. But this is the book, and the visible work showing on it proves how difficult it is to write and edit a work.*

In addition to writing the first draft of new chapters, Jim would be taking time to rework earlier sections to accommodate changes that had been suggested, so that his attention was continually split between writing, revising and doing further research, all within the same time frame. This complex assortment of activities required skillful orchestration:

*When one has a manuscript as long as this one, as intricate, and as closely inter-locked in its parts, the loss of even one page can be devastating. I have therefore always followed the practice of allowing not one page to be removed without making a note of where it has gone. I do this on slip sheets of cheap yellow paper and insert them to represent the missing pages. I cannot relate how helpful this has been and how confused and mixed up I would often have been without them. Sometimes, in the preparation of the manuscript, I had segments of it (1) with Erskine, (2) on the way to Erskine, (3) with Nadia being typed, (4) on the way to Nadia to be typed, (5) on the way from Nadia to Erskine, (6) with Kings or Dalton or Laird to be edited, (7) with any one of a dozen experts to be read for accuracy. Only the most careful mothering of this flock of papers enabled me to hold them together in some form or other.*

It was a jigsaw that appealed to Michener's love of intricate detail, and often when he was not sorting out the comings and goings of his very lengthy manuscript, he would turn for relaxation to those maddeningly difficult cube and block assembly puzzles designed to perplex the most deductive minds. Of the many he tried, then passed on to confuse us, there was only one he failed to solve.

Michener wants there to be enough information in his novels for readers to find them just as viable in 25 years' time. He writes them to last, and he says exactly what he wants to say, irrespective of whether some readers will want to stay with him all the way. His early chapters on the formation of the land and its first inhabitants were of extreme importance to him. He knew full well that his readers might find them tough going, but they were essential parts of his comprehension of the total span of the novel, and there was no way he would consider abbreviating this portion of the book. He felt that all chapters were essential stones in the total arch of *Centennial*, that although they covered radically different ground they were nonetheless interlocking elements, each contributing to, and dependent on, their neighbors.

When the final first draft of the novel was completed, Michener left Denver to work with his publisher, Random House, for a long period of editing and revision before he felt satisfied that there could be no further improvement in the manuscript. To confirm the overall authenticity of a finished manuscript he normally invites a highly qualified authority to read and report on it from as critical a standpoint as possible. *Iberia* was vetted by Dr. Kenneth Vanderford; *The Source* went to Eli Misrachi, Secretary of the Israeli Cabinet; and *Chesapeake* to Dickson Preston. But for *Centennial* this procedure did not apply. Sections of the book, on specialized subjects such as the geology, ancient animals and early man, were submitted to various eminent authorities, but the total manuscript was not sent to any one person. Michener felt confident that our combined knowledge and the depth of our research were sufficient for him to dispense with this routine. Quite apart from that, it would have been difficult indeed to find one person versed equally in the preparation of souse, the cropping of sugar beets and the proliferation of the dinosaur.

*Centennial* was published in October 1974, and quickly became Michener's fastest-selling novel since *Hawaii*. In essence it had taken him thirty-eight years to write, and when asked whether he himself appeared in the book, he said: "In this novel the grizzled old bison, Rufous, comes rather close to representing me."

When we had researched all the rivers in *Centennial*, we went on a mainly recreational foray to parts of the west Jim had grown to love some forty years earlier. Once again, as in so many areas we had covered, it was a river that fascinated

him most. This time the mighty Colorado, photographed here
in Glen Canyon National Recreation Area, Utah, captured
his imagination. "More than on any other river in America,"
he said, "I would like to write about the Colorado."

# CHAPTER V

# THE FILM

arly in August 1977, to break a hot and seemingly endless 430-mile car journey from my home in Big Horn, Wyoming, to Denver, Colorado, I stopped in Cheyenne to touch base with Randall Wagner, Director of the Wyoming State Travel Commission, an old friend who had been very helpful to Michener on several of our research trips into southern Wyoming. From Randy, I learned that two Hollywood producers, Howard Alston and Mack Harding, had called at his office the previous day, August 11, to seek help in finding possible locations for a television film version of *Centennial*.

My initial excitement that someone — three years after the book's publication — had summoned the courage and imagination to translate the 900 complexly inter-woven pages of Jim's western odyssey into visual terms for the television screen was replaced almost instantly by a sense of anxiety. How could outsiders who had had no part in its creation hope to interpret the story successfully? Emotionally I had travelled every mile of the long trail from Horsehead Crossing on the Pecos River. I had suffered the many ups and downs of the Crown Vee outfit. I had experienced storm, drought, the Depression. In my mind's eye I had a clear vision of all the scenes, and I knew each character in *Centennial* intimately. How could someone else's ideas possibly approach the intent of the original?

My mind roller-coasting with conflicting reactions of thrill and fear at the news, I drove on to Denver, only reaching some equilibrium of thought when I recalled Jim Michener's practical and philosophical attitude toward films made from his books. Of some fourteen movies of his work, only *The Bridges of Toko-Ri* had translated successfully, from his point of view. In early years the sometimes pathetic inadequacy of these screen versions had infuriated him, yet he had always refused to involve himself in film treatments, though he had several times been invited to participate as a scriptwriter.

"It's a whole other skill, another world of which I know little, although it has always fascinated me," he explained when I had queried the film potential of *Centennial* during its writing. "I never think about film possibility when I'm writing a book. The requirements of a film are entirely different. I always hope for a good translation

Barbera Carrera as Clay Basket, Pasquinel's Indian wife, with their daughter, Lucinda (Brandyn Woolrab). (Photo © Tessa Dalton)

to the screen, but in the final analysis, when all the films of my books have been made, and most of them forgotten, the books themselves will still be there, with their stories intact as I intended them. Remembering that has saved me a lot of anguish over several unacceptable movies that have been made from my novels."

Now the object of the exercise was to be *Centennial,* and remembering Jim's attitude could well save me from a lot of frustration and heartache. Before the manuscript was finished, it had become obvious to me that the only way to handle it on film would be as a TV series, episode by episode, and that no single 120-minute movie-screen adaptation of it could possibly transmit its power and scope. Early in 1973 I had suggested to Hobart Lewis, of *Reader's Digest,* that his TV division consider its possibilities. Lewis's editors offered that it presented such difficulties from a script point of view as to be virtually untranslatable into television terms. I dropped the matter. The book would only come alive at the hands of some imaginative fanatic determined to *make* it work. From that time I had heard nothing of film possibilities until my visit to Cheyenne.

On my return from Denver to Big Horn, I telephoned Jim, who confirmed that there were negotiations but that, to the best of his knowledge, nothing had yet been finally decided. He was too engrossed with his new book, centered upon the history of Chesapeake Bay, to let his mind be diverted more than briefly to the film potential of *Centennial.*

Bit by bit the situation became clearer and Jim's involvement and interest much more positive. Universal Films had plans to translate *Centennial* into a minimum of 13 and possibly as many as 25 hours of viewing time. NBC was to be the network, John Wilder, of Universal, the executive producer. These were the bare bones of the situation. Later I was to learn that Frank Price, as president of Universal Films' television division, had optioned the book in the hope that some format could be devised to bring it successfully to the TV screen. Price had virtually pioneered the translation of long novels into successful television serials. Through him, *Rich Man, Poor Man* became the first novel to be televised at length and to score heavily in the ratings.

His enthusiasm for the book was matched by Wilder's almost obsessive interest in Jim's panoramic view of western history. When *Centennial* was first published, John Wilder was totally absorbed as producer of the successful *Streets of San Francisco* series, and his wife Carolyn's entreaties that he read Michener's book went unheeded until she went straight for his heart with her plea: "John, you just *have* to read this book, it's all about your own family's background."

That did it, for Wilder had always been fascinated by the story of his own great-great-grandfather's wagon trek from Illinois to Puget Sound, Washington, in 1852. He began *Centennial* and was soon reading it aloud to Carolyn, word by word, from start to finish. "The similarity of incident on the wagon trek was almost uncanny," he says. "My ancestor, Sherwood Bonney, wrote the following passage in his journal:

> *I sacrificed my land for $1,000, bought two wagons, six yoke of oxen, two cows and provisions for the journey.*
> *We were in good health, and in high hopes we started on that tiresome journey for the far west on the 7th April, 1852. Our route lay on the north side of the Platte River."*

During that trip Bonney's wife died, his brother died, his four-year-old son died, but he reached Puget Sound, opened the first school in Pierce County, Washington, in 1854, and took up a homestead on American Lake, Washington, in 1876. "I spent the first five years of my life in that homestead," added Wilder, "and wherever I went after that I carried with me an almost fanatical curiosity about the pioneering of the west. Now *Centennial* was bringing it all to life for me."

When Frank Price, eager to bring John Wilder to Universal, offered him the chance to produce Michener's novel, the fates were orbiting in their rightful trajectory. "It's the one project above all others that I'd like to work on," Wilder told Price, and he shortly began the task of translating Michener's text into 25 hours of acting script.

That work had been going on through the summer, and around the time I stopped in Cheyenne, John submitted the first three hours of script for Michener's comment. Wilder wrote: "I have been anxious to write since beginning the adaptation of *Centennial* in March, but decided it best to complete the opening screenplay first. I hope it reflects my love for the book and my desire to be faithful to its tone and intent . . . I hope I can do justice to the translation. I'm sure going to give it everything I have."

Wilder suggested a meeting with Jim, and waited anxiously for a reply, which was delayed by Michener's usual pressure of commitments. Almost one month after submitting the first script Wilder received this letter:

*1 September 1977*

*Dear Mr. Wilder,*

*This letter is not an adequate response to yours of 9 August 1977.*

*But out of courtesy to a fellow writer, I must hurry this off to assure you that I have read through page 36 — that is past the end of Act One — and am delighted with what I find. You have a fine sense of the west, a feeling for Indians, and a good hand in bringing things to a climax dramatically.*

*I thought your pace was about right for the difficult opening. I'm on camera about two scenes too much, but that can be adjusted. I was afraid, from reading first the cast of characters, that you might be omitting the formation of the land, and judge that you have done it about right, providing for some great photography and diagrammatic material.*

*At any rate, we're on course and I'll report further when I've finished the entire. I will do this prior to leaving for Spain, and will endeavor to write briefly before then. I'll be back home about October 1 and would be most pleased to meet with you, but it will not be possible at this time to travel to California, which I would normally do out of respect for your working schedule. My schedule is set by others right now, and I must obey.*

*Most congenially,*
*Jim Michener*

This letter could hardly have been more encouraging, and Michener followed it up with a second, barely one week later:

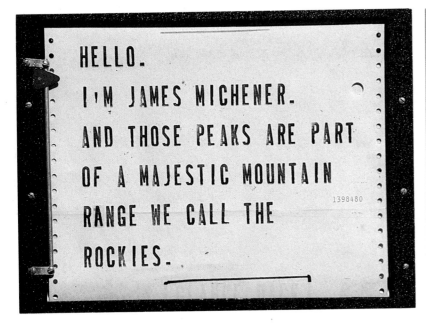

HELLO.
I'M JAMES MICHENER.
AND THOSE PEAKS ARE PART
OF A MAJESTIC MOUNTAIN
RANGE WE CALL THE
ROCKIES.

1398480

The opening words of TV's 25-hour journey through *Centennial*.
John Wilder, Executive Producer and scriptwriter of the movie, discusses a point with Michener. Time: 7 am; location 13,000 feet up, on top of the Tetons.

Filming the opening narration of the television film version of *Centennial*, made by Universal for NBC. Michener, in orange jacket, begins to tell the story, against a backdrop of Wyoming's great Teton range.

*Dear Mr. Wilder,*

*I have now finished the script and find it excellent. I have been especially pleased with the invention of new incident to bridge what you were using precisely of mine, and what had to be adjusted to accommodate flow.*

*I liked your use of more dialect with McKeag, but feared that some of his speeches might be too long. However, what he said sounded good.*

*I was especially pleased with the sleeping scene in which the two men meet. This read extremely well.*

*I like the device of the narrator very much, for these early episodes; I'm not too sure that it should be continued into the latter ones. But the arbitrary break at scene 429 seems exactly right to me, and well written.*

*Some of the St. Louis scenes with Gaillard seemed too talky, but I do not visualize well what the camera can do to liven such material. I felt this dragged a little. But the concluding pages were very good, established some solid material for future use, and ought to play well.*

*Most warmly,*
*Jim Michener*

Michener was now beginning to pay close attention to Wilder's work, at a very difficult time when he was completing the writing of his new novel, *Chesapeake*. It was indication enough that he felt the odds to have been considerably shortened in favor of *Centennial*'s being well translated into the medium of television; and his association with the project — and with John Wilder — became closer as it progressed.

Independently, I read the screenplay and found it excellent, sensitive and staying very close to the original story line. Such changes as there were had been mainly created to bridge arbitrary chapter breaks in the book, which of course have to be handled differently in a visual rendition, and to establish areas of continuity in the action of the main characters. Some minor, yet significant, incidents attributed in the book to less important protagonists in the story were realigned to be part of the experience of the principal players — a device of Wilder's that was entirely consistent with adapting the written word to the needs of the screen. All in all, the portents were so good that the adrenalin of hope began to rise sharply.

At the beginning of October, John Wilder called to ask if I thought Michener would come out west within a few days to narrate the opening sequence of the television treatment. The filming proper would not start until February 1978, but it would be finished by fall, ready for prime-season viewing, so this was the only chance to shoot Michener against a backdrop of western mountains drenched in the glow of autumn. "We think a location near Durango, Colorado, would be fine," he told me. "We'd need him for two or three days at the most, but I really want to get the fall colors into the scene."

Alas, when I called Jim he was about to incarcerate himself with Albert Erskine to work on the newly completed first draft of his Chesapeake Bay novel. "I'd like to do it, but tell John Wilder it will have to be after the week ending October 15. From then on, my time is yours."

I knew that when he and Albert hole themselves up in Connecticut nothing can stir them, so Wilder and I began a guessing game as to whether the leaves would still be on the trees by the time he came out, for the onset of winter in the west is fickle, and the combination of a parched summer and an early withering storm could strip his lovely scene overnight. We toyed with an alternative location further south in the Sangre de Cristo range that pokes into New Mexico from southern Colorado, but decided to play the whole thing by ear until the last minute.

Around the 10th Wilder called again to say that his associate producer, Howard Alston, now preferred an earlier suggestion of mine, that the sequence be shot in Teton National Park against the backdrop of the Tetons. "But there'll be no colors at all left there now," I protested. "Jackson had a severe early winter storm just a few days ago. Besides, there's no knowing what kind of weather we'll run into if we choose that location. It can change from Indian summer to blizzard within hours."

Wilder was insistent that the dramatic Tetons, rising abruptly from the floor of Jackson Hole, now far outweighed his former preference for flaming autumn foliage. "We're going for Jackson," he told me. "If, at the last minute, the weather fouls up, we'll switch the crew to Durango. Ask Mr. Michener if he could come to Denver on Sunday, October 16, and we'll start work in the Tetons on the 17th." He suggested I invite Mari along, too, and to arrange for Tessa Dalton, who was now working in Denver, to join the group.

The new plans suited Jim, who is so philosophic about the logic of filmmakers that any proposed location, short of the moon, would not have surprised him. "Mari and I will be there. Ask Tess to meet us in Denver and we'll fly to Jackson together." John Wilder, who had never been to Wyoming, planned to bring his wife, Carolyn, along, too.

The weather stayed fair, day after day, and on the 15th Wilder confirmed that Jackson Hole would, indeed, be the setting for Jim's opening narration. I had arranged to go over by car, and on the 16th I drove in the crisp early-morning air across the uplands of the Big Horn mountains, from Sheridan, and headed toward Yellowstone Park and the Tetons. I had arranged for us all to stay at John Turner's Triangle X Ranch, near Moran Junction, where we had spent a night on the field trip to research the mountain-men section of *Centennial*. Nearly four and a half years had passed since then, and as I drove across the great arid basin of Wyoming, now bereft of the summertime campers and trailers that throng the highway like ants, going back and forth to Yellowstone Park, the years between telescoped. This weekend, though this time in a very different way, we were once again on the road in search of *Centennial*.

In Cody, Buffalo Bill's preferred wallow, I passed the supper club that prompted Michener's terse dismissal of Wyoming's gastronomy. "I've travelled in most parts of the world," he said after suffering nobly an onslaught of meat and liquor that would have turned back a stevedore, "but from here on I pray I may be spared Wyoming supper clubs!"

From Cody, I drove past the raggle-taggle clutter of tourist distractions that mar the otherwise superb scenery of Wapiti Valley. As I left the lower valley behind and climbed to the seclusion of Yellowstone's protected kingdom, thin skeins of early snow lay on the higher ground, and the great expanse of Yellowstone Lake glinted in the midday sunlight. No ice yet, not even along the water's edge, but soon this entrance to the park would be sealed by winter snows, and the lake be solid ice, twenty

Sketches for costume designs, by Helen Colvig. Reproduced through permission of Universal City Studios, Inc., Universal City, Cal.

In a scene shot on a cold and rain-swept day,
Pasquinel prepares to leave his Arapaho friends.

Robert Conrad, as Pasquinel, begins the long
journey down the South Platte to the Missouri,
his canoe loaded with beaver pelts for the rich
St. Louis market.

miles from shore to shore. Today, seagulls still screeched above this quasi-ocean, and flocks of duck and Canada geese crowded the inlets and ponds that fringe the great lake.

Leaving the south entrance to the park, I reached Jackson Lake, at the foot of the Tetons. The Tetons are like no other range I have ever seen, and each time I go to Jackson, at whatever time of the year, I am always caught unaware by the invasion of their beauty. From whatever direction you travel, suddenly there they are before you, without any warning, their marching spires surely one of earth's most eloquent creations. No other mountains in the world can have been photographed as much — probably a minimum of 10,000,000 shots each year. Now, in the steps of *Shane,* a western "great," shot in this same setting, we had our own man to match the mountains. We were going to photograph Jim Michener against that scene-stealing backdrop.

As I reached Jackson Hole airport, the little Cessna 210 ferrying Michener from Denver was already making its approach circle to the north of the landing strip. The skies were blue and benign to the point of absurdity, not a cloud to portend those vicious storms that at this time of the year can turn the valley into a swirling white tempest.

The Cessna swung off the runway and braked to a halt at the charter hangar, and Jim's head appeared through the hatchway, covered with typical inappropriateness in a tweed deerstalker's hat. Behind him were Mari, Tessa Dalton festooned with cameras, and associate producer Howard Alston. Jim climbed into my car for the 15-mile ride to Triangle X, and within minutes was discussing the logistics of the filming, very much interested, but with a cool hand on the throttle of anticipation. "I've learned never to be too excited by this sort of thing, and I don't want you to get your hopes too high, either," he counselled. "There are so many factors in the film world that can pre-empt the best intentions. I wouldn't count on anything at this stage, but it will be interesting, and we'll have fun doing it." Five years before, at the outset of the *Centennial* research, he had used that same phrase, "We'll have fun." Then, scared of the weight and reputation of James A. Michener as a relentless taskmaster, I had rejected that possibility. Today, in the warmth of this reunion, and with the memories of many humorous moments during the making of the book, I had no doubt that we would find pleasure in this latest journey.

For three days an almost festive atmosphere prevailed. The Wilders brought their four engaging children, and John and Jim Michener were at once at ease with each other. Within minutes of our arrival at the Triangle X, John Wilder suggested that we take a quick look, before dinner, at one or two possible locations for the next day's shooting, an idea that appealed at once to Jim, who is always unsettled by an idle moment. In the warm glow of the early-evening sunlight we scouted Glacier Gulch overlook, the clear air sharpening the shadows on the face of Grand Teton and making the 7,000-foot ascent from the valley floor look no more than a strenuous ramble. Only the distant sound of the wind scouring the 14,000-foot peaks above the totally windless calm where we were standing reminded us that the ascent of Grand Teton is for professional climbers only — however idyllic conditions may appear from a distance.

We moved on to the sequestered, gentle beauty of Jenny Lake, its dark, unruffled waters at the foot of Mount Owen reflecting the surrounding pines. Then to String Lake, a mere capful of water and the smallest of the seven lakes along the face of the range. Finally to the overlook at Willow Flats, with the broad, squared top of Mount Moran dominating the wide waters of Jackson Lake. On the flats, a cow moose in the distance foraged with her leggy calf, while a coyote ranged the nearer meadows, his nose dictating a winding course in pursuit of supper. We left and went in search of our own.

Next morning we went to work after an early breakfast, joining the camera and sound crews busily setting up equipment for the first day's shooting at the glacier overlook. The filming of the opening three-minute sequence of 300 words spoken by one person, Jim, took three days, 21 Universal personnel, seven vehicles and a helicopter to perfect — and I was assured by John Wilder that it was a very small crew by movie standards. It was soon easy to understand why so much time needed to be allotted for such an apparently small task. By the time the camera dolly had been placed on two 2 x 10 planks laid on the sage scrub ground and levelled with various wedges, by the time angles, distances, metering, zoom techniques and lighting of Jim had been worked out to satisfaction, by the time the sound equipment had been tested, and the boom angled correctly over Jim's head, by the time the traffic had been halted on the road, and we had waited for the drone of a plane from the airport to clear the sound range, and by the time Jim had been rehearsed in where to walk, when to walk, where to start speaking, to look, to stop speaking, we were ready for the first take.

The camera panned the glorious mountain backdrop, came round to Jim Michener, then moved along the dolly track in unison with Jim's walk to a rock mark, where he would stop and speak. At the precise moment he began to say, "Hello, I'm James Michener," spoken into the immense silence and beauty of the scene, a wheel on the dolly squeaked. "Cut," yelled the director.

Nothing could make the wheel stop squeaking, no oil, no powder, no persuasion, none of the jokes, none of the swearing, no realignment of the track. Next, the light changed and the mountains became flat and bland and hazy and there was no point in trying to cure the wheel, anyway.

At best it had been a rehearsal for the following day. At 7:30 the next morning, after a spectacular sunrise that painted a soft rose-red band along the mountaintops while the lower ground was still reaching for light, we rode the Jackson Hole aerial tram from Teton Village to the top of 12,000-foot Rendezvous Mountain, to shoot a breathtaking sequence of the Teton peaks from their own level. It was cold, but sunny, with a wind-chill factor dropping the temperature to around zero. There was no camera dolly up there, only a tripod, so no squeaks broke the enfolding silence of that barren, crenellated wilderness. Michener, bolstered against the cold in a borrowed pair of blue woollen long-johns, spoke his lines without fault:

> "I suppose my primary reason for writing the book I called Centennial was to ask us . . . you and me . . . if we're aware of what's happening right now to this land we love . . . this earth we depend on for life.
>
> "It's a novel, of course, and its characters and scenes are imaginary. There was no Venneford ranch, no prairie town of Line Camp, no Skimmerhorn cattle drive in 1868 . . . no town of Centennial. On the other hand, certain background characters are real . . . and the work couldn't have been created without the cooperation and conclusions of many eminent historians."

Michener with Virgil Vogel, Director, on
location east of Greeley, Colorado.

Rendezvous of the mountain men, filmed at Estes Park, Colorado. (Photo © Tessa Dalton)

Robert Conrad, with Jim and Mari Michener
in the background, trying to keep warm on a
chilly, rain-soaked day along the South Platte.

Clint Walker, Richard Chamberlain, and Robert Conrad between scenes on the St. Louis waterfront.

By 10:30 we were once more on the floor of the valley, driving to Signal Mountain, a sizeable hill rising from the floor of Jackson Hole at its northern end near Moran Junction. From its summit, reached by a winding road, Wilder wanted to shoot a sequence against the background of the mountain-girt valley. On the road from Teton Village we played a Michener word game, a reminder of the tantalizing brain-nudgers he devised to while away the miles during our *Centennial* research trips. "Three words, 'tremendous,' 'horrendous,' and 'stupendous' end in 'dous'" he said. "What is a fourth?" At Signal Mountain, I passed the problem on to others. Jim snoozed on a bench in the sun while the film crew wrestled both with the equipment and the teaser. At one point during the shooting John Wilder took me urgently aside, and I thought we must have a crisis on our hands. All he wanted was to plague me for some kind of clue to the answer. At one point the dolly, now cured of its malaise, rolled off the plank, but was rescued at the start of what could have been a hazardous downhill journey. Wilder was far more interested in the fourth word than the fate of that ill-starred dolly.

Again Jim spoke his lines well, and several of the "takes" were marked "Print":

> *"It's a big story. About the people who helped make this country what it is . . . and the land that makes the people what they are. And it's a story about time. Not just as a record . . . but also a reminder. A reminder that during the few years allotted to each of us, we are the guardians of the earth. We are, at once, the custodians of our heritage . . . and the caretakers of our future. I hope you'll find the time to live with us the adventure of the American west."*

The day had gone well. That evening Wilder showed us a portfolio of the costumes proposed for *Centennial*'s leading characters. The sketches were beautifully rendered in watercolor and Universal's costume designer, Helen Colvig, had not only suggested appropriate and historically accurate clothing, but had drawn them on her own interpretation of the physical proportions of Michener's cast. For the first time, size, weight, features, and coloring were replacing the concepts of one's imagination. As Wilder turned the pages, wistful Elly Zendt, merchant Bockweiss, Pasquinel, trail boss Skimmerhorn, Lame Beaver, Lucinda, McKeag, and hapless Oliver Seccombe came to life, clearly and vibrantly.

That half-hour spent with Jim's western family increased our confidence that a fine team had been put to work on *Centennial*. Wilder told us that the costume department's enthusiasm for the project was typical of reaction generally at Universal to the making of the film.

On the final morning, Wednesday 19th, Wilder reconvened us at the Glacier Gulch overlook, the scene of our first morning's fiasco. This time everything went smoothly, the mountains sharp against the faultless blue sky, and Michener, now utterly relaxed, turning on like a pro. "Hello, I'm James Michener," he said for the 57th time,

> *"and those peaks are part of a majestic mountain range we call the Rockies. It's hard to imagine them disappearing from the face of the earth, isn't it? And yet they did disappear once . . . only to be formed again. Not the very same mountains, of course. But formed in roughly the same spot . . . and from many of the same rocks.*

He begins to walk, paralleling the peaks . . . and the camera drifts with him . . .

> *"When a mountain ten thousand feet high vanishes over a period of forty million years . . . it means that each million years it loses two hundred and fifty feet. Which means that each thousand years it loses three inches. And the loss per year is so small, it can't possibly be detected while it's happening."*

And that was it. The opening sequence was now in the can. Wilder and his Universal crew pulled out of Jackson that afternoon. Jim, Mari, Tessa and I were left behind to enjoy a last evening at the Triangle X. At dinner we shared a table with the only other two guests now remaining at the ranch, a large, quiet woman and her equally unassuming, though far less ample, husband. Jim and Mari made several attempts to include them in our conversation. We were in good form, going over the last three days, discussing when we might next meet. At one point, to make the reason for our visit clear, Mari explained to the wife that Jim was the author of a book called *Centennial*. "Oh, really," said the large lady. "I must try to read it when it comes out."

Nothing daunted, Mari charmingly redoubled her efforts to include the couple. Turning to the husband, she enquired his line of business. "I'm in plastics," he offered, "and we're here from New Jersey." Ah! At last an opening for Jim, who is always keen to hear of the skills and expertise of other people's livelihoods. "What particular line of plastics are you in?" he asked. "I make the molds for a wide range of products."

This was not enough for Jim, who always likes to narrow down to the fine points. "That must be very interesting," he ventured, "but I imagine you specialize in some particular type of plastics?" We all looked up. A long pause. "My particular field is enema nozzles and douche tips," the husband said quietly. It was the only time I have ever heard Jim fail to press for fuller details of a man's vocation. He didn't even ask what color.

Next morning I drove Jim, Mari and Tessa back to Jackson airport, ready to leave on a charter flight at 8:00 a.m. to make the Denver connection to the east. The skies were finally clouding over, a gray and wintry blanket blocking out the Indian-summer sun we had enjoyed for the past three days. The plane took off and headed in an easterly direction — back toward the salty implications of Chesapeake Bay.

Michener's collaboration and friendship with John Wilder grew steadily after this first meeting. Wilder is the type of working professional Jim admires, in this instance a compact, eager, modestly assertive 42-year-old who could be mistaken easily for a lightweight boxer in good condition. In 1973 he received nomination as author of the Outstanding Teleplay of the Year, and in 1974 as Producer of the Outstanding Dramatic Series of the Year — both being for his work on the *Streets of San Francisco*. This combined talent for scriptwriting and for producing had now brought him to Universal as executive producer and scriptwriter of *Centennial*, the most exciting challenge of his career.

On his return from Jackson Hole to Maryland, Jim was quick to follow up his meeting with John Wilder, in a letter that shows his keenness to focus in closely on the film interpretation. The second line of the first paragraph forced a cry of dismay from Wilder before he read to the end of the sentence, but by the time he reached the signature he knew he had Jim's close interest in his efforts:

127

Augusta, Kentucky, became an authentic setting for the
early St. Louis waterfront scenes in *Centennial*. Towns-